A Time to Grow

A Time to Grow

Lenten Lessons from the Garden to the Table

KARA EIDSON

First edition
Published by Westminster John Knox Press
Louisville, Kentucky

22 23 24 25 26 27 28 29 30 31—10 9 8 7 6 5 4 3 2 1

Book design by Sharon Adams
Cover design by Lisa Buckley

Library of Congress Cataloging-in-Publication Data

Names: Eidson, Kara, author.
Title: A time to grow : lenten lessons from the garden to the table / Kara Eidson.
Description: First edition. | Louisville, Kentucky : Westminster John Knox Press, 2022. | Summary: “This Lenten study explores the thematic elements of gardening and eating to connect faith to food as we slow down, grow, and celebrate with feasting on Easter Sunday. Additional elements include sermon prompts, liturgies, altar art ideas, and prompts for children’s time during worship”—Provided by publisher.
Identifiers: LCCN 2021046367 (print) | LCCN 2021046368 (ebook) | ISBN 9780664267049 (paperback) | ISBN 9781646982271 (ebook)
Subjects: LCSH: Gardens—Religious aspects—Christianity—Meditations. | Gardening—Religious aspects—Christianity—Meditations. | Lent—Meditations.
Classification: LCC BV4596.G36 E33 2022 (print) | LCC BV4596.G36 (ebook) | DDC 263/.92—dc23/eng/20211015
LC record available at https://lccn.loc.gov/2021046367
LC ebook record available at https://lccn.loc.gov/2021046368

In memory of

Hoyt and Margaret Owsley, who taught me to love the earth;

Waldo and Francis "Tank" Eidson, who taught me to love food;

Arlene Johnson, who taught me how to grow food from the earth;

and all five, who taught me that loving God happens through loving others

Contents

Introduction

*T*he inspiration for this Lenten resource comes from two of my greatest passions, faith and food—particularly, the growing and tending of my own food. When I am in the garden with my hands in the earth, I feel deeply connected to creation, and thereby more connected to God, our Creator. Through stories of gardening and food, I hope to invite you into that space where you also may grow more connected to God. Whether you are a Master Gardener or struggle to keep houseplants alive, we are all united in our need for sustenance; we all need food.

And at the heart of every human celebration, we find food. It is the common thread of the human experience. Nations, religious traditions, even individual family units all share their own special set of uniting rituals—and a majority of these take place, in some manner, around the idea that food and bounty ought to be shared. Whether it is breaking the Ramadan fast, enjoying a wedding feast, surrounding a grill on the Fourth of July, participating in the Eucharist, gathering together for Passover, or even participating in the simple tradition of cake and ice cream at a birthday party, our celebrations and the foods we consume at them are deeply intertwined.

However, due to agricultural industrialization and mass urbanization, many of the connections to the creation of our food have been lost in the short span of one or two generations. A few years ago, I was picking strawberries at a pick-your-own strawberry patch near our home. (We grow enough strawberries in our garden to eat, but not enough for making jam or doing any serious canning.) I was sent to a row near a couple in their mid-thirties who had brought their kids to the patch, and they were discussing strawberry harvesting. The young father began asking the farm's owner about strawberries.

"How are strawberries harvested in bigger operations?" the young man asked.

A little baffled, the owner responded, "The same way you just harvested them."

"Wait. You mean someone has to pick every strawberry I see in the grocery store?"

"Pretty much," the older farmer replied.

There are pictures of me picking strawberries in my grandfather's garden that predate my earliest memories, and I remember helping my family harvest corn, green beans, tomatoes, and more. For a long time, I took for granted the knowledge that those experiences also provided. But many people in my generation, and the generations that follow, have not shared this experience. They have seen combines harvesting things like feed corn and wheat, so they do not know that machines are not capable of harvesting most of the produce we consume.

Many of my clergy colleagues, raised in cities and suburbs, also tend to lack this experience—despite the fact that many of us end up serving older, rural congregations of people who were raised on farms or make their living in agriculture. Exploring where our food comes from has the potential to unite disparate generations whose experiences are vastly different from one another. I have yet to meet a person raised on a farm who does not eagerly share barnyard stories from his or her childhood, and these stories tend to delight even the most ardent city dwellers. I have yet to encounter a young child who does not eagerly dive into the earth when given the chance to plant or explore.

I was concerned when I was sent to my first rural appointment. Raised in the suburbs of Kansas City, I knew that nothing in my time as an associate pastor at an urban and (extremely) liberal church had prepared me for the experience. Little about my chaplaincy experiences in a downtown Kansas City hospital matched the reality of my congregants. Nothing about my four years working with college students prepared me for the rural, aging, small church. I had spent the past four years staying as current as possible on pop culture, a job requirement when working with college students. My new congregation was openly skeptical of my education, my age, my vocabulary, my gender, and even my attire. My decision to wear dress pants one Easter was based on the sleet pouring down outside; it never occurred to me that a woman in pants on Easter would be considered scandalous in the twenty-first century.

They liked hunting; I have shot a gun once in my life, and it was a BB gun. They had trucks for farming; I had a fuel-efficient Honda Civic to save money on my long commute. They had lived in the same community their entire lives; I had lived in seven different communities just in the last ten years. They liked the privacy of country living; in my entire life, I had never lived more than a five-minute drive from a grocery store. They considered a good vacation to be going to see their grandchildren; I considered a good vacation traveling halfway around the world to scuba dive four or five times a day. Many of them believed no good movies had been made since John Wayne died, but he died before most of my favorite movies had even been created: *Harry Potter*, *The Hunger Games*, *Star Wars*, you name it. (I have still never seen a John Wayne movie.) Some of them had great-great-great grandchildren; married but childless, I had just turned thirty.

How on earth was I going to connect with these people?

I mean, there's always Jesus. But what about sermon illustrations? What about small talk? Then I found it. I found what we had in common. A childhood spent harvesting produce in my maternal grandfather's garden and visiting my paternal grandparent's dairy farm had instilled in me a connection to the earth that went beyond a general love of food.

It seemed like a small start, but it was a beginning. We started swapping recipes, discussing creative solutions for the overabundance created by a single zucchini plant. We began sharing gardening successes and failures, and I remember the look of surprise on one woman's face when I offered up a solution to her dilemma of blossom-end rot on her tomatoes. After I built a chicken coop in our suburban backyard, we began trading crazy chicken stories. In a group of people with whom I had little else in common, I had found my "in."

The authenticity of these connections mattered and was not something I could have faked my way through, mostly because a conversation about manure and composting practices is an admittedly difficult topic to discuss with feigned passion. Having lived a suburban existence for much of my life, I found that these conversations also helped connect me to my roots, both figuratively and literally.

In the modern United States, we live in a world of fast food and to-go meals, where many people have forgotten the fundamentals of where food comes from. Within this culture, we have lost one of the uniting factors of what makes us human: the simple act of breaking bread together. Journeying through the season of Lent with this in mind, we can slow down, move through the painstaking process of growth, and end together with great feasting and celebration of the resurrection on Easter morning.

While growing or preparing food may not be at the heart of each of the Scripture passages in this study, you will quickly see how each story tells who we are as a Christian people. In the same way, our favorite foods—the ones we really and truly love—tell a story about who we are as well. I hesitate to use the cliché, but "we are what we eat."

Even in urban areas, popular culture has once again begun to recognize the value of reconnecting to our food and its origins. Millennials who consider themselves "foodies" shop at farmers markets, pay more to "buy local," and frequent restaurants that advertise themselves as "farm to table." Part of this is my generation's desire to make the world a little better—the recognition that how our food is produced and shipped can have massive impacts on our environment and is a matter of social justice for fellow human beings. But I think part of the appeal comes from a deeper desire to put down our screens and simply be together over food that is as good for our bodies as it is for our souls.

Whether your church is in the city center or in the heart of farm country, I believe you will find a way to connect with this Lenten experience. After all, we all eat. There are infinite factors contributing to what we eat and how it is prepared: culture, geography, nationality, religion, socioeconomic status, tastes, and food allergies or aversions. The way we eat varies: seated around a table, positioned behind the wheel while sitting in traffic, walking down a street, perched on tall barstools at a counter, or rushing between meetings or while chasing a toddler. Our bodies require sustenance. The incarnation of Christ teaches us that our bodies matter to our Creator. God cares that we are embodied.

This resource includes reflections and a study guide for small groups to use during the season of Lent, or by individuals during their own private Lenten journey. The sections are divided by the Holy Days in Lent, which include Ash Wednesday, Maundy Thursday, and Good Friday in addition to each Sunday of the season. There are discussion questions at the end of each section. While it is unlikely small groups will have a meeting for every Holy Day during Lent (especially as there are three in Holy Week alone), these questions can still be used for personal reflection and be discussed the next time the group meets for conversation. Each section also includes brief daily devotionals for each of the forty days during the Lenten season, placed between each longer reflection. A few of the daily devotions are poems. Contemplate these during your devotional times on those days. If poetry just isn't your thing, consider how you could rewrite the day's poem to turn it into your own personal prayer for the day.

If you are using this resource with a small group, consider these options for enhancing your experience of this study together:

- Invite a local farmer to come to your group and discuss why local farming matters. If you don't know any farmers in your area, contact a local CSA (community supported agriculture) or a local farmers market organizer. They will put you in contact with a farmer who would love to speak to your group.
- Take turns preparing and hosting a meal for the group each week.
- Make each gathering a potluck. Have each group member bring a dish with a special story, and ask them to share the stories (and maybe even the recipes) over the food at the beginning of your time together.
- Meet one week in a group member's garden. If there are no gardeners in your group, ask around your church.
- Find a local farmers market to attend as a group. Consider creating a meal together with the items you find there.
- Ask a local farmer if the group can meet at their farm one week. If the farmer is willing, ask the farmer to give you a brief tour and explain how the farm operates.

Preachers and worship leaders can use these readings and the accompanying questions to inspire their sermon preparation for a worship series that brings the whole congregation into the experience of *A Time to Grow*. Worship series materials in the back of this book include liturgy with communal responses, altar art ideas for decorating worship space, prompts for children's time in worship, and a communal spiritual practice for the entire congregation during the season of Lent. All references to Scripture use the New Revised Standard Version of the text and are drawn from the assigned Lenten readings across years A, B, and C of the Revised Common Lectionary.

We begin with dirt on Ash Wednesday, exploring the very soil from which we have come and to which we will return. The theme for each week will guide us through the elements of the garden: soil, order, life, water, light, restoration, time, remember, fast, and feast. We will journey through the intricacies of how faith is required to produce food and how that faith can lead us all to feast at the table on Easter morning. The art of growing and preparing food is more than simple sustenance; it is an opportunity to come together in community and share in abundance. Consider this your personal invitation on a journey from seed to table—your invitation to pull up a chair at God's heavenly feast.

Ash Wednesday

SOIL

Joel 2:1–2, 12–17; Matthew 6:1–6, 16–21

Blow the trumpet in Zion;
  sound the alarm on my holy mountain!
Let all the inhabitants of the land tremble,
  for the day of the LORD is coming, it is near—
a day of darkness and gloom,
  a day of clouds and thick darkness!
. . . .
Yet even now, says the LORD,
  return to me with all your heart,
with fasting, with weeping, and with mourning;
  rend your hearts and not your clothing.
Return to the LORD, your God,
  for he is gracious and merciful,
slow to anger, and abounding in steadfast love,
  and relents from punishing.

Joel 2:1–2a, 12–13

"Whenever you fast, do not look dismal, like the hypocrites, for they disfigure their faces so as to show others that they are fasting. Truly I tell you, they have received their reward. But when you fast, put oil on your head and wash your face, so that your fasting may be seen not by others but by your Father who is in secret; and your Father who sees in secret will reward you.

"Do not store up for yourselves treasures on earth, where moth and rust consume and where thieves break in and steal; but store up for yourselves treasures in heaven, where neither

> moth nor rust consumes and where thieves do not break in and steal. For where your treasure is, there your heart will be also."
>
> Matthew 6:16–21

Cultivating Soil

As any gardener or farmer can tell you, the most important part of growing anything is starting with the right soil. The devoted grower can give a seedling the perfect conditions of water and light, but if the soil is bad, nothing will grow. To the outsider without a microscope, except for a couple of earthworms, a bare patch of soil appears to be dead and lifeless. In a lot of ways, this is true. Soil is largely comprised of decomposed matter from formerly living things. However, the best soil also teems with life (microbes, good bacteria, worms, etc.). What appears dead is a living thing.

In most places, the cultivation of good soil requires a great deal of care and attention. There are a few exceptions to this rule, but for the most part, healthy soil doesn't just happen—it requires work. Earth needs to be properly turned over or tilled, the right nutrients need to be added, and crops need to be rotated. Sometimes soil even needs a season of rest to restore and replenish—farmers refer to this as letting a field "lie fallow."

Industrialized agriculture has led to mass soil depletion across the United States.[1] In order to continue producing plants on this depleted soil, mass agriculture must add large amounts of chemical fertilizer (which is not conducive to human health or the health of our planet). Simultaneously, vast quantities of animal manure are washed into our watersheds every day. This is both a waste and an environmental tragedy; my favorite fertilizer in my garden is the manure produced by my chickens.

My husband and I recently moved, and while we were excited about our new house and land, we were sad to leave behind our peach tree, blueberry bushes, blackberry vines, and strawberry patch. However, our real grief stemmed from leaving behind the soil in our garden. We had worked hard for ten years to create the perfect growing environment in our raised garden beds—composting, adding chicken manure, turning things over by hand, and cultivating the perfect environment for worms. The soil in those garden beds was the result of years of hard work, using techniques that modern technology might lead us to forget.

I observed one such method for fortifying soil when visiting my grandparents, long before I understood what I was witnessing. My grandparents didn't have a garbage disposal. For a long time growing up, I thought the bowl sitting next to their sink to collect food waste (peels, inedible portions of fruit and vegetables, eggshells, etc.) was simply a way to reduce the amount of trash that had to go to the curb. When I was growing up, all of that stuff went down the garbage disposal at our house. While I understood that the bowl at my grandparent's house was emptied onto a compost pile, I didn't understand that this was one way my grandfather improved his garden. I didn't understand that all the "waste" was being recycled back into the ground. I also didn't know, until much later in life, that every few years he would clean out a friend's horse barn and then work those massive amounts of horse manure into the soil of his garden, thereby fortifying it for yet another few seasons. And so, in a tradition that skipped a generation, my husband and I have been composting at our house for quite some time now. The addition of chickens to our home stepped up our composting—they produce excellent fertilizer. The results speak for themselves; each summer and fall we reap another bountiful harvest.

Composting at home or in our churches significantly cuts down on what goes into our landfills. When food is deposited in landfills, it does not receive enough oxygen to break down in the same way it will in a compost pile, and it produces massive amounts of methane, a greenhouse gas. Composting can help cut down on a family or a community's carbon footprint.[2]

I went through a period of incredible spiritual darkness a few years ago. One day my spiritual director asked me if I could think of an image for what I had learned through that dark time. My response? "Chicken shit." She looked a little taken aback. I assured her, "That's the image—chicken shit." My chickens produce a lot of waste. Every few weeks I remove their waste and place it on the compost pile. If I place it directly on the garden, it will kill everything right away. But if I remove all that manure, let it rest for six months, and then apply it to the garden, I likely won't have to put fertilizer on that patch of garden for the rest of the year.

The spiritual lesson I was sharing with my spiritual director was this: Beautiful and bountiful produce grows, quite literally, out of shit. Through God's grace, beautiful and bountiful things can grow out of life's most horrible moments, even the moments that are absolute shit. Sometimes those moments can turn into the most beautiful spiritual fertilizer we can imagine. As the chorus of Lisa and Michael Gungor's song "Beautiful Things" expresses, "You make beautiful things out of dust, you make beautiful things out of us."[3]

We have become detached from the natural order of the world. We place chemicals we can't even pronounce on our plants to make them grow while we shun the most basic designs in nature. Livestock create, as natural by-products, some of the best fertilizer available. Many talented gardeners I know who garden in the city still get cow patties (lumps of dry cow manure) from their friends in the country and steep the cow patties in water. It goes by different names (my husband's grandmother calls it "manure tea"), but these excellent gardeners water their garden with the liquid produced from this combination. Raised in the suburbs—I'm a "city girl" through and through—I would have once turned up my nose at cleaning up after my chickens. I loved the idea of keeping chickens in my backyard, but I was hesitant about the prospect of shoveling all that manure. When I realized that chickens produce gardening gold (in addition to their nutritious eggs), it completely changed my attitude.

Barren Soil

At our old house there was a patch of bare earth in the backyard for almost eight years. Despite my husband's tireless administrations, we never successfully grew any grass in that back corner by the fence. Since we don't know the entire history of that little piece of land, there are a million things that could have been wrong with the soil back there. One spring I had an idea. I went out with a shovel and turned over the entire corner of the yard where nothing would grow, and then I flung handfuls of wildflower seeds across the entire area. We figured that nothing else had grown back there; we didn't have anything left to lose. Much to our surprise, the wildflowers took root, and that back corner of our yard was the most beautiful part of our garden that summer.

Sometimes our lives feel a lot like that soil: a barren patch void of life, where nothing good will grow. We have all felt that way at one time or another. This is part of the cycle of the human experience.

On Ash Wednesday we are called upon to lay bare our souls. We are called to recognize the stark reality of human existence: "From dust you have come, and to dust you shall return." Not only do we repent of our sins and cry out to God in anguish, but we mark religiously that we are made of dust and that one day our very bodies will return to the soil from which they have come.

Every year, I offer ashes at the back of the sanctuary or worship space with the traditional language, "From dust you have come, and to dust you shall return." But I also remind the congregation prior to this time that the word "repent" literally means "to turn around." After they receive ashes at the back of the sanctuary, I invite them literally to turn around and receive the grace of Communion at the front of the church. It is a beautiful way to give people the sense of physically turning around as they are called to spiritually turn around as well.

The prophet Joel is unique among his prophetic counterparts. There are only a few prophets that historians are unable to place based on historical context in their prophecy, and Joel is among those few. The book seems to have been written after the exile, after the people of Judah have returned from Babylon; however, there are not enough clues in the text to give a definitive answer on the time frame. Additionally, while many of his prophetic counterparts emphasize repentance as turning away from evil and toward justice, Joel's focus on repentance is concerned with turning toward God in worship. Joel calls for the blowing of the trumpets because the day of the Lord is coming near—and in Joel's prophecy, the coming of the Lord is not a good thing. But Joel warns the people that they may be spared the wrath of God if they turn toward God in communal worship.

The text makes clear that the precipitating event for Joel's prophecy was an ecological disaster, followed by an economic one (a simple "a + b = c" equation in an agrarian society). A great plague of locusts devastated the harvest, and the land was left in crisis. While some prophets lay a charge against the people of Israel for a specific unfaithfulness that led to their calamities, Joel's prophecies make no such accusation. Instead, the overarching theme of Joel is a call to the people to draw closer to God by gathering together and worshiping as a community.

Motivations Matter

Joel calls for communal repentance—an idea foreign to many twenty-first-century American Christians. When there is an accusation that something in our culture is racist or sexist, there is always at least one individual too quick to jump up and exclaim, "But I'm not racist" or "I'm not sexist." True, perhaps that person might not be racist or sexist, but that doesn't mean that that same individual might not profit and benefit from societal practices that are racist and sexist.

We encounter this same challenge with Jesus' words for the day. All too often when the Matthew text is read, the hypocrite about whom Jesus speaks immediately becomes the "other." Other people are the hypocrites, not us. Jesus is inviting the hearer to hold up a mirror and see the places where practiced piety is about appearances rather than true holiness. How do we live out our faith for the appearances others see, and how do we live out our faith in authentic and genuine ways? Jesus is not speaking to the "others"; he's speaking to the "good people." (The Pharisees, though often maligned by modern Christians, certainly thought of themselves as "good people," as did their contemporaries.) Jesus is saying that living life so that others will see us as "good people" is not enough, that motivations matter.

The Communion service that accompanies this book, heavily adapted from The United Methodist Church's Service of Word and Table, has some difficult moments of repentance. It acknowledges that we are participants in corporate sin. The food on our tables often makes us guilty participants in this corporate sin. From the sin of food deserts in our inner cities, to minimum wage workers being unable to afford fresh produce and healthier food, to the mistreatment of migrant workers who harvest vast quantities of the produce we consume, to the ways in which agricultural practices destroy both the environment and the financial well-being of the farmers who are just trying to get by, we are all called to repent of our complicity in a food system wrought with sin. In the "Order" chapter of this book, you will find some suggestions for ways we can change our behavior so that we might, in some ways, remove ourselves from some of these sinful systems. This liturgy might make you and other members of your church uncomfortable. Embrace the discomfort. That is what Ash Wednesday is for—an honest look at ourselves, an honest look at our own sins and hypocrisies, and coming together to take steps toward embracing repentance and wholeness in both the Creator and in God's creation.

From dust we have come, and to dust we will return. But never fear—God makes beautiful things out of dust.

QUESTIONS FOR REFLECTION AND DISCUSSION

1. Have you seen God turn manure into something beautiful in your life? What was that experience like?
2. What knowledge did you already have about soil cultivation and health? What did you learn? Did anything surprise you?
3. Does your congregation compost? Why or why not? Do you compost food waste from your own home? Why or why not? How could composting be a spiritual practice for your congregation or family?
4. Have you had moments where your soul has been laid bare? How have those moments shaped you? How have those moments changed you? How has God worked through those times in your life?
5. What does the prophet Joel's call for repentance look like in our era? In what corporate sins do you recognize your complicity? How can we participate in communal repentance in the twenty-first century?
6. What does the practice of Ash Wednesday mean in your spiritual journey?

DAILY REFLECTIONS

Thursday

As this series begins, find a windowsill in your home where you can set a small planter. Plant some seeds in potting soil and watch them grow. Consider how God might be calling you to growth during this Lenten season. What changes might God be calling you to make during these forty days? How might you be called to repentance during these forty days? As you tend to your seedling, consider your journey each day.

Friday

Spend ten minutes today doing some research into how you might compost in your setting. What sort of compost bin would you need in your kitchen, your yard, your apartment? Would composting be a viable option in your home? How can we reduce our impact in landfills, taking better care of God's creation, through the practice of composting? If you have a garden or lawn, how might they benefit from your compost?

Saturday

Today's devotion is the first poetry devotion. When you encounter the poetry devotions, take time to meditate over them for the day. If poetry isn't your thing, consider how you might rework the themes of that day's poem into your own personal prayer.

> *Dust*
> From dust I have come,
> to dust I will return.
> Scientists tell me
> most elements in my body
> have come from a star.
> I am literally stardust.
> So, what else can a Creator like that do?

First Sunday of Lent

ORDER

Genesis 2:15–17; 3:1–17; Luke 4:1–13

The LORD God took the man and put him in the garden of Eden to till it and keep it. And the LORD God commanded the man, "You may freely eat of every tree of the garden; but of the tree of the knowledge of good and evil you shall not eat, for in the day that you eat of it you shall die."

. . . When the woman saw that the tree was good for food, and that it was a delight to the eyes, and that the tree was to be desired to make one wise, she took of its fruit and ate; and she also gave some to her husband, who was with her, and he ate. Then the eyes of both were opened, and they knew that they were naked; and they sewed fig leaves together and made loincloths for themselves.

They heard the sound of the LORD God walking in the garden at the time of the evening breeze, and the man and his wife hid themselves from the presence of the LORD God among the trees of the garden. . . .

To the man he said,

> "Because you have listened to the voice of your wife,
>   and have eaten of the tree
> about which I commanded you,
>   'You shall not eat of it,'
> cursed is the ground because of you;
>   in toil you shall eat of it all the days of your life."

Genesis 2:15–17; 3:6–8, 17

Jesus, full of the Holy Spirit, returned from the Jordan and was led by the Spirit in the wilderness, where for forty days

> he was tempted by the devil. He ate nothing at all during those days, and when they were over, he was famished. The devil said to him, "If you are the Son of God, command this stone to become a loaf of bread." Jesus answered him, "It is written, 'One does not live by bread alone.'"
>
> Luke 4:1–4

Garden Mapping

My husband and I lived in our first home for ten years. After a long search, we finally purchased a new house on ten acres. While some people might spend vast amounts of energy planning decorations and color schemes for a new home, I spent endless hours plotting and planning our new garden. In fact, part of the reason our search for the perfect house took as long as it did was because the lay of the land on which the house was built was so important to us. We found one house that we loved, but all of the flat parts of the property that would have been ideal for gardening were bordered by enormous trees on the neighbor's land to the west. Why does this matter? Our garden would not have had full sun, meaning that it would have been in the shade for a significant portion of the day. There are very few foods that grow well without full sun, so this property was not an option for us.

Order matters greatly in the life of the garden. I can't just go out in my backyard, throw out some seeds in the spring, and expect to be canning tomatoes in late August. Every year, we draw a map of what will be planted and where it will be planted. Something that loves heat, such as sweet potatoes, can replace other crops that mature early in the season, such as regular potatoes or leafy greens. Certain plants will be finished by midsummer and will allow us to plant more fall crops in those spaces. Rotating what we grow is always important from season to season—we don't want to deplete the nutrients in the soil. There are many factors to consider: sun exposure, drainage, fertilizer, and weather patterns of that particular year. Cages and supports must be provided for the tomatoes, new blackberry vines must be tied to a trellis to keep them from growing out of control, fruit trees must be trimmed, strawberries must be mowed over when they stop producing, and strawberry plants must be carefully covered with a thin layer of straw after the first frost. The order of all things is vital to the health and life of the garden.

Time and time again in Scripture, we hear God's call to order the life of humankind: God calls us to choose the way that leads to life—in other words, to choose the way that leads toward the giver of all life. In scriptural terms, sin equals death. Sin is anything that turns us away from God, and anything that turns us away from the Divine is the opposite of life-giving—it is death-giving and death-dealing.

Even in the names of characters of the story in Genesis we find the deep connection to the earth that gives us life. The name "Adam" comes from the Hebrew *adamah*, which means "earth" or "soil." It is wordplay on the fact that God forms Adam and Eve from dirt, as a potter molding clay, and then God's breath turns these two shapes of dust into living beings. When we say, "From dust you have come and to dust you shall return" on Ash Wednesday, part of this comes from the idea that God forms human beings out of the dust of the earth.

Furthermore, Eve's name in Hebrew is also wordplay on the Hebrew word for "life." As the mother of humankind, she is recognized as the giver of all life. As Diana Butler Bass points out in her book *Grounded*, the first two human beings are essentially named "dirt" and "life."[4] We are foolish to overlook this reality—from the dust of the earth all life emerges. Even strict carnivores are dependent upon this reality.

In Disney's *The Lion King*, the young cub Simba has a conversation with his father Mufasa. Mufasa is training his son to become the next king, and tells him, "Everything you see exists together in a delicate balance. As king, you need to understand that balance and respect all the creatures, from the crawling ant to the leaping antelope." Simba interrupts his father and asks, "But don't we eat the antelope?" Mufasa gently tells his son, "Yes, Simba, but let me explain. When we die, our bodies become the grass, and the antelope eat the grass. And so we are all connected in the great circle of life." Creation is intended to fit together, creating this circle between dirt and life, a cycle that repeats again and again.[5]

Ordered Creation

The order of creation is not by accident. An abundance of scientific research informs us that the shortcuts we try to take are bad for us: high caffeine consumption may keep us alert but is an unhealthy alternative to good sleep. We try to cheat on calorie intake by drinking artificial sweeteners, while study after study tells us of the detrimental health impacts of such sweeteners. We take a multivitamin in the morning and think that is a satisfactory substitute for our nutritional needs. The list goes on and on. I'm grateful to live in the twenty-first century; without access to modern medicine, I would have died at least four or five times over. But there is something to be said for the lives lived by many of the "Greatest Generation"—growing food for the family in a garden, freezing and canning that food for the winter, and considering produce that couldn't be grown in one's own region to be a "special treat." (When my parents told stories of receiving oranges on Christmas as a special treat, I thought this sounded like a terrible gift. There were oranges in the grocery store every week of the year by the time I was growing up in Kansas.)

Not long ago, in the middle of a cold April, someone told me she had gone to our local farmers market and was extremely disappointed. "There wasn't a single strawberry or blueberry in sight! No fruit at all!" she complained. I reminded her that the vendors at our local farmers market can only sell what has been grown locally, and that everything was behind schedule in such a cold year. Even in a warm year, there wouldn't be any kind of berries at the market for at least another month. "But they have all that stuff at the grocery store!" she replied. "It's been there all winter!"

How easily we take for granted that the grocery store will be stocked year-round with produce that has been shipped in from South America, Mexico, California, and all sorts of places warmer than our locale. A basic understanding of growing seasons and climate considerations is no longer common knowledge in our culture. When it comes to buying produce in the United States, for the most part, if we can afford it, we buy it any time of the year. We have disrupted the order of the natural world by shipping produce halfway around the globe. We choose to ignore the order of the seasons, and in doing so, we pay the price for the carbon footprint of global shipping.

Adam and Eve chose to eat the fruit of the tree of the knowledge of good and evil, despite God's warning that they would die when they did so. They disrupted God's order in the world. And while they did not die the day they ate it, they began the slow journey toward death with that act. The lectionary intentionally pairs the fall of Adam and Eve with the temptation of Christ in order to highlight Jesus' role as the new Adam and the new Eve, in that Jesus demonstrates what Adam and Eve could have been. Genesis tells the story of humanity's fall away from the divine bringer of life, but Jesus' resistance to temptation demonstrates how life can be found in reliance on God. Jesus is the antithesis of the fall and shows by example how we might all avoid temptation to sin.

Defining Sin

In today's passage from Luke, Jesus is tempted to sin. And what is sin? I hear this question a lot. It is one of those "churchy" words that gets thrown around all the time, but even people who sit in the pews every Sunday may struggle to define such a basic concept. The simplest definition of sin is anything that draws us away from God. In the context of order, sin is anything that disrupts our inclination to stay in relationship with God and God's creation. I have found that this basic definition of sin is often a source of frustration for people—especially young people. People often want a much less nuanced explanation, desiring a more black-and-white response to the question "Then what actions are sinful?" Their frustration is understandable, because this definition requires more reflection, nuance, thought, and work than a list of "thou shalt" and "thou shalt not."

Here is a classic example that I often use in conversations about sin. I do not believe it is inherently a sin for an adult to have a glass of wine with dinner or a beer at a sporting event. However, if that adult has a history of alcoholism, that single drink could certainly constitute sin—the disruption of that person's relationship with God and others. Likewise, a person having multiple alcoholic beverages and then getting behind the wheel of a car is certainly sinful. The consumption of alcohol is not inherently sinful—but under certain circumstances, it certainly can be.

We choose to live outside of the order of God's creation at our own peril. Moral guidelines—those things that keep us from sin—do not exist because God is punitive. They exist because God is loving and wants us to be in right relationship with God and with others. The order of creation was designed for living beings to thrive. When we attempt to align ourselves with God's created order, we take a step toward closer communion with both God and our neighbors.

Is it a sin to eat produce out of season? Of course not. Is it a sin to eat produce that has made a long journey to our table? I hope not, because I would never eat citrus fruit or a banana again if I limited myself to things that can be grown exclusively in my region. But it is impossible to deny that the system by which we acquire most of our food is full of sin. It's outside the order of creation.

Many small and medium farmers in the United States have been driven out of business by industrialized agriculture—giant corporations that are rarely connected to the communities in which the actual farmland is located. The overreach of industrialized agriculture has also led to many U.S. farmers using unsustainable practices in the desperate attempt to keep their family businesses operational. The stress on farmers is so great that in 2018, after three members committed suicide, one dairy co-op sent out suicide prevention materials with the farmers' monthly milk payment.[6]

In the current agricultural market, sellers and buyers tend to be primarily concerned with appearance and ship-ability of produce, resulting in products with less nutritional value. Many small farmers and migrant workers are taken advantage of in the name of profit, creating vast human rights violations throughout our food production system. Many consumers completely ignore what is locally in season, vastly increasing the carbon footprint of food production because it is shipped halfway around the world. "Food deserts" in our major cities have created highly populated areas that are completely devoid of fresh produce. As a result, we are all, by nature of what we consume, a part of a system racked with sin.

Reordering the World

God calls us into the work of reordering, endeavoring to restore God's original order in creation. We can begin this work by choosing what we eat with more care. A simple way to eat what is in season and support local farmers is to sign up for a local CSA (community supported agriculture) in your area. Most CSAs are operated by local farmers and provide customers with in-season produce from their farms once a week. There is a bit of a gamble with this approach in that there is no guarantee what will be in the bag each week. You may wind up with produce you are initially uncertain how to use, but almost all the farmers I know are more than happy to share a recipe or two of their favorite way to eat what they grow. If getting to a farmers market weekly is not a viable option, this can be a wonderful way to still support local agriculture. Some CSAs also offer meat, milk, or egg options.

While cost can often be an issue with eating local, many farmers markets offer some sort of "double your dollars" program for those who participate in the WIC food program (formerly known as "food stamps"). These participating markets allow people to as much as quadruple their WIC dollars, benefiting the individuals in the program with healthy food while also further supporting local farmers. When looking at how much more expensive local meat can be, my husband and I decided that we would try to eat local meat but eat less meat in general.

American cities and rural areas have swaths of land where food deserts exist. These are locations where people live but where it is difficult (sometimes impossible) to obtain fresh food and produce, most often because grocery stores do not operate in the area. In cities with dense populations, trying to get something as simple as an apple or a gallon of milk may require driving several miles, which presents an incredible challenge to individuals who do not own a vehicle. There may be any number of shops or gas stations within the food desert, but it is rare for these locations to offer anything other than processed foods.

Many organizations are already at work trying to change these food deserts, especially in metropolitan areas. Initiatives to help close food gaps include community gardens, mobile produce stands, and co-ops in effected neighborhoods. Most of these organizations are only too happy to receive new volunteers, or even partner with church communities.

One of the simplest ways to improve our relationship with creation is through being better stewards of the food we consume. The USDA estimates that up to 40 percent of food produced in the United States is never eaten.[7] While a lot of this waste occurs long before the average consumer encounters the product, we can still do our part to be better stewards of the food that ends up in our homes and on our plates. A change as simple as making an effort to consume leftovers can make a difference in the burden food systems place on our planet's resources.

We are not a completed work, and God is not done with us yet. We are called to do the hard work. Barbara J. McClure summarizes the work of Rabbi Rami Shapiro, who offers these words of hope: "Do not be daunted by the enormity of the world's grief. Do justly, now. Walk humbly, now. You are not obligated to complete the work, but neither are you free to abandon it."[8]

QUESTIONS FOR REFLECTION AND DISCUSSION

1. How does order matter in a garden? How does order matter in how Christians structure their lives? What does your plan/map look like?
2. What is the significance of the names "Adam" and "Eve"? How does understanding the meaning of their names impact your understanding of the text?
3. We all take shortcuts in life. What shortcuts do you take concerning the order of creation? How might these have negative impacts on your health, your life, or your soul?
4. Do you know what is locally available in various seasons in your geographical region? If not, do a quick internet search. Are there things that surprise you? How might you and your congregation commit to eating more locally?
5. How do you understand sin? How do you understand repentance and reconciliation with God?
6. In what ways might you reorder your life to more fully align with God's intended order for creation?

DAILY REFLECTIONS

Monday

At the heart of the creation story, God creates order out of chaos. I used to feel resentment for all the "rules" that come with the Christian life. But I have found, with time, that the order of the Christian life is just that: order. We ignore the order of God's world at our own peril. God's order is not that of a vengeful oligarch—it is that of a loving parent, trying to create a healthy environment for a beloved child. How have you ignored God's order in the past? How might you live into God's order in the future?

Tuesday

There is a reason that keeping a Sabbath day made it into God's "major orders" of the Ten Commandments. God knows that our bodies, minds, and souls require rest. Consider the order of your week. When do you find time to rest, time to spend with God, time to relax? Our culture values productivity highly, and many things we choose to do during our downtime are not fully life-giving (social media, mindlessly watching television, etc.). How might you find more restful and life-giving options for the quiet moments in your life? Even fields and gardens need periods of rest to be at their most productive.

Wednesday

Spend ten minutes today researching local agriculture in your area. Most likely there are CSAs available in your area. These vary with location and season, but joining one is an amazing way to support local farmers and feed your household. It may entail picking up a few new recipes along the way. For example, Swiss chard, rhubarb, parsnips, and sweet potatoes were not part of my culinary heritage; I had to learn what to do with those ingredients. But now some of my favorite dishes contain three of those four items. Learning to eat what is in season is a behavioral challenge but can also be viewed as a spiritual challenge—a way to be faithful to our Creator and what our earth can provide.

Thursday

Today, find some time for centering prayer. If you don't have a preferred centering prayer, use this suggestion. In between each line, take ten deep breaths, slowly in and slowly out. If you are someplace private, say each line out loud.

> Be still and know that I am God.
> Be still and know that I am.
> Be still and know that I.
> Be still and know that.
> Be still and know.
> Be still and.
> Be still.
> Be.

Friday

What was yesterday's centering prayer like for you? Was it challenging to pray so slowly? Was it difficult just to be still and just to be? Christians tend to be very good at asking God for things, and even at offering up prayers of thanksgiving, but we often are not as skilled in simply spending time with God. Consider the relationships in your life. Healthy human relationships require that we spend time with the people we value. Slowing down to meditate or to practice centering prayer is how we spend quality time with God.

Saturday

> *Divine Order*
> I hate lists.
> Too much order fails to account
> for the occasional necessity of napping.

But in the kitchen, I measure
to the gram, the ounce, the teaspoon.
In building the chicken coop, I measure
to within a fraction of an inch.
In the garden, I carefully consider the angle
at which the sun will fall on blueberry plants
after five more years of growth.
Somehow, God's order always sneaks in.

Second Sunday of Lent

LIFE

Genesis 15:1–12, 17–18; Mark 8:31–38

After these things the word of the LORD came to Abram in a vision, "Do not be afraid, Abram, I am your shield; your reward shall be very great." But Abram said, "O Lord GOD, what will you give me, for I continue childless, and the heir of my house is Eliezer of Damascus?" . . . He brought him outside and said, "Look toward heaven and count the stars, if you are able to count them." Then he said to him, "So shall your descendants be." And he believed the LORD; and the Lord reckoned it to him as righteousness. . . . On that day the LORD made a covenant with Abram, saying, "To your descendants I give this land, from the river of Egypt to the great river, the river Euphrates."

Genesis 15:1–2, 5–6, 18

Then he began to teach them that the Son of Man must undergo great suffering, and be rejected by the elders, the chief priests, and the scribes, and be killed, and after three days rise again. He said all this quite openly. And Peter took him aside and began to rebuke him. But turning and looking at his disciples, he rebuked Peter and said, "Get behind me, Satan! For you are setting your mind not on divine things but on human things."

He called the crowd with his disciples, and said to them, "If any want to become my followers, let them deny themselves and take up their cross and follow me. For those who want to save their life will lose it, and those who lose their life for my sake, and for the sake of the gospel, will save it. For what will it profit them to gain the whole world and forfeit their life? Indeed, what can they give in return for

> their life? Those who are ashamed of me and of my words in this adulterous and sinful generation, of them the Son of Man will also be ashamed when he comes in the glory of his Father with the holy angels."
>
> Mark 8:31–38

Fully Alive

In my elementary school science class, we planted a bean in a wet paper towel inside some plastic wrap. When it sprouted, we were able to watch it grow. We studied it each day and monitored its progress. I was fascinated by this secret of the universe being revealed before my eyes. I had planted seeds before. I had been told by my teachers or caregivers that a plant would emerge from the dark and mysterious depths of the soil below. But by the time the adult in my life pointed out to me that a sprout had emerged from that dark place, I had already forgotten we had planted a seed. This time, with only a paper towel and plastic baggie between me and the seed, I could see the sprout's slow progress from day to day, long before it would have emerged from the soil. I felt like all the secrets of life were unfolding before my eyes.

Life is miraculous, and God has created us to live abundantly. Born nearly one hundred years after the death of Christ, the church father Irenaeus wrote that "the glory of God is [the human] fully alive." Unfortunately, what makes us fully alive spiritually is not in alignment with what the world tells us leads to abundant life. Culture and human nature consistently teach us that whoever has the most toys wins. When we surround ourselves with items and comfort, we give ourselves a sense of safety and success, but this is a vastly different approach to life than the lessons we learn throughout Scripture.

People living in certain parts of the world (such as the United States) are used to having easy access to what we need and want. Prior to the COVID-19 outbreak of 2020, I never had trouble finding anything I needed, and what I wanted (within budget constraints) could usually be procured easily with a quick online search and fast shipping. But suddenly, as the world realized the outbreak had become a pandemic, certain items were in short supply and high demand. Some of these are things I would have expected to see shortages of during a pandemic: disinfectant wipes, face masks, safety gloves, bleach. Other item shortages caught me off guard: bread flour, brown sugar, dishwashing soap, and—most importantly—toilet paper.

A lot of this was panic buying. One friend confided in me that as the shutdown was looming, he went to the grocery store in a panic. He loaded his cart with far more than he could possibly use in a week, largely because he saw everyone else in the store doing the same. At one point, he dumped what remained of the store's supply of sugar-free drink mix into his cart; a year later, he still had drink mix in the pantry that his family has grown tired of. In a time of potential scarcity, my friend looked around him and saw other people hoarding resources, so his instincts told him to copy their behavior. Despite being a person of impeccable logic, he still caved into the hype of panic buying.

There was an illusion that an abundance of goods might save us from what was a terrifying and completely unknown virus. None of us believed that canned goods could keep us from getting sick, but many people (myself included) stocked up on what they could when they realized scarcity was a possibility. We bought into the myth, even more than usual, that an abundance of possessions would lead to an abundance of life.

Realigning Expectations

All too often, abundant life in God looks very different from our expectations of how the world ought to be ordered, or our perceptions of how the world has been ordered. There are frequently times when a gardener must perform tasks that seem completely counterintuitive to the end goal of abundant life. Tomato plants are one of the more delicate items in the garden, and as such, it is best to grow seeds indoors and under grow lights until they are established enough to expose to the elements outdoors. Tomato seeds are miniscule, and short of using tweezers and a microscope, or expensive and elaborate farming equipment, it is nearly impossible to plant one or two seeds per cell (a cell is an individual space on a growing tray). As such, multiple seedlings will sprout in one cell, which necessitates thinning for optimum growth. This means the gardener must judiciously (and I will admit, sadly) pick perfectly healthy seedlings out of the tray to discard, to make room for one or two plants to grow successfully. Crowding of plants will not result in successful growth, so thinning is an absolute necessity. What seems counterintuitive is necessary for success; the gardener must realign expectations to sustain successful life.

Similarly, Abram and Sarai were forced to realign their personal expectations to align with God's. Ancient Hebrew tradition did not maintain a belief in an afterlife. As such, there was a consistent belief that success in life meant an abundance of offspring; people could live forever through many descendants. Abram and Sarai shared these expectations and beliefs, and as they continued to grow older with no children, they began to believe they would not have an abundance of life.

Abram and Sarai had spent their lives in a tribal social system, and the dangers of leaving one's tribe were great. At this juncture in human history, most historians estimate the average human being never ventured more than ten miles from his or her place of birth. In a more recent historical analogy, it is similar to people who migrated from Europe to North America in the eighteenth and nineteenth centuries, knowing they would never again see their loved ones left behind. There was no returning if a beloved family member became ill. There was no going back for birthdays, special occasions, or funerals. Parting with loved ones under these circumstances was not dissimilar to a death.

Abram and Sarai's leap of faith is a drastic one. They leave behind the only life they have ever known in the hopes of living into God's promise that their descendants will become more numerous than the stars in the sky. After entering into covenant with God and being renamed Abraham and Sarah, they continue to age without children of their own. Eventually, they are forced to realign their perspective on abundant life: even just one heir will fulfill the promise. When Isaac is born, they find this abundant life in realigning their perspectives on what constitutes "enough."

Give It Away

While we see the paradox in Sarah and Abraham realigning their expectations for abundance in the joy of one child, Jesus also frequently speaks in paradox. Mark 8:35 is a prime example: "For those who want to save their life will lose it, and those who lose their life for my sake, and for the sake of the gospel, will save it." Too often, Christians have done a disservice to new converts to the Christian faith. A premise is offered as bait: if you accept Jesus Christ into your heart, your life will become better and easier—but this is a false premise. I do believe following Jesus Christ will make a person's life better, but the "easier" part couldn't be further from the truth. Jesus spells it out in this passage from Mark: we must give up our lives to save them.

My maternal grandparents had two sons and two daughters, and each of those four children married and had children of their own. In their retirement years, my grandparents dedicated a lot of their time and energy into feeding their children and grandchildren through the garden. I remember rows upon rows of canned green beans, canned tomatoes, blackberry jelly, and strawberry preserves lining the shelves in the storage cupboards in each of our respective homes. But in addition to caring for their own family, they often took boxes of fresh produce and canned goods to church and encouraged anyone in the community to take what they needed. My grandparents worked tirelessly for large portions of the year to grow, produce, and store all this food, only to give most of it away, frequently to unrelated people from the community. They understood and lived into the paradox that it is more life-giving to give than to keep everything for oneself.

The life of the gardener is one of hard work, producing life to sustain life. Cultivating food for the table is not without its blood, sweat, and tears. There is the toil of turning over soil, digging holes for planting, carefully weeding a garden throughout a season, braving the high heat of summer to care for the garden, tending to daily watering, and prepping a garden at the end of one season for the beginning of the next. It can be easy to forget the hard work that goes into food production when much of our food comes shrink-wrapped, waxed, and immaculately clean, but whether food comes from a garden or a grocery store, there are many hours of hard work behind it.

The hard work of gardening mirrors the hard work of altering our expectations of abundance to align with God's expectations. It is common for Jewish people to use the expression *L'chaim* at a celebratory gathering. Translated into English the phrase means, "To life." It is most frequently used as a toast, and because it is always used in the marriage service, it has become closely tied with that ceremony. Disregarding the world's expectations for what makes life abundant is not easy work, nor is realigning our expectations for abundance with God's. But we are called to wake up each morning and say, "Today I choose to turn my face toward God. Today I choose the path that leads to abundant life. Today I choose to seek the Giver of Life in all things. Today, to life!"

QUESTIONS FOR REFLECTION AND DISCUSSION

1. Irenaeus writes, "The glory of God is [the human] fully alive." What does being "fully alive" mean for you?
2. When have you experienced times of abundance in your own life? When have you experienced times of scarcity? How did these experiences impact your relationship with God and with others?
3. Where did you encounter scarcity during the COVID-19 pandemic? How did it impact your life? Your perspective? Your faith? How did these experiences realign your own expectations and understandings of abundance?
4. How might you realign your cultural understanding of abundance with God's understanding of abundance? How can this lead to more abundant life?
5. Imagine yourself doing what Abram and Sarai are called to do. What is it like? What does it mean to be called to something new in life?
6. How must Jesus' followers give away their lives in order to save them? What might God be calling you to give away?

DAILY REFLECTIONS

Monday

I don't have children of my own, but I have observed that many friends and family members feel completely overwhelmed in the first few days and weeks of parenthood. One friend reflected, "I couldn't do anything but take care of the baby, nurse, and sleep. Nothing else was getting accomplished around the house. So I had to keep reminding myself: I kept a tiny human alive today, and that is enough." New life is messy and demanding; Abraham and Sarah discover this twice—once when they start a new life in the promised land, and a second time when they become parents in their old age. Name some moments when new life has felt overwhelming for you. Has your faith community supported you in those difficult times? How has God supported you in those moments?

Tuesday

I don't know anyone who was fully prepared for the COVID-19 pandemic that swept the world in 2020. Life as we knew it shut down in the United States and across large swaths of the world. But I was struck by how much of life still went on. Nothing was normal—and yet the natural world went on as normal: spring arrived, seeds needed to be planted, flowers sprang forth, my chickens began laying eggs again, and my husband's bees were happily harvesting all the pollen they could collect. Despite our belief that "everything was canceled," creation was still operating in terms of its "regularly scheduled programming." What might we learn about God's abundant creation in chaotic times?

Wednesday

The summer my husband was studying for the bar exam, he also started his own sourdough bread starter. Committed to this effort, he cultivated wild yeast from apples, and for the first week he even got up every few hours during the night to feed the sourdough starter. Ten years later, we are still enjoying bread from that same starter. Are there times when you have sacrificed something in your life for the long-term future? How has your faith played a role in these moments?

Thursday

The song "Words to Build a Life On," written by Mike Crawford and His Secret Siblings, contains the lines "Blessed when the plans that you've so carefully laid, end up in the junkyard, with all the trash you've made."[9] When has your life taken unexpected and unplanned turns? How has God been at work in these moments of anguish and broken dreams? Where have unforeseen blessings arisen through tragedy and despair?

Friday

Read the following verse several times slowly. Consider it carefully and make it your prayer for today.

> See, I have set before you today life and prosperity, death and adversity. If you obey the commandments of the LORD your God that I am commanding you today, by loving the LORD your God, walking in his ways, and observing his commandments, decrees, and ordinances, then you shall live and become numerous, and the LORD your God will bless you in the land that you are entering to possess. But if your heart turns away and you do not hear, but are led astray to bow down to other gods and serve them, I declare to you today that you shall perish; you shall not live long in the land that you are crossing the Jordan to enter and possess. I call heaven and earth to witness against you today that I have set before you life and death, blessings and curses. Choose life so that you and your descendants may live, loving the LORD your God, obeying him, and holding fast to him; for that means life to you and length of days, so that you may live in the land that the LORD swore to give to your ancestors, to Abraham, to Isaac, and to Jacob. (Deut. 30:15–20)

Saturday

Green Hope
The seedlings break forth from the dust,
green hope bursting into new life.
The greatest magic—seed to plant—
takes place beneath the dust,
in realms of dark mystery.
We, too, begin and end in the dark.
From dust you have come,
to dust you will return.
But God does amazing things with dust.

Third Sunday of Lent

WATER

Psalm 63:1–8; John 4:5–42

O God, you are my God, I seek you,
  my soul thirsts for you;
my flesh faints for you,
  as in a dry and weary land where there is no water.
So I have looked upon you in the sanctuary,
  beholding your power and glory.
Because your steadfast love is better than life,
  my lips will praise you.
So I will bless you as long as I live;
  I will lift up my hands and call on your name.
My soul is satisfied as with a rich feast,
  and my mouth praises you with joyful lips
when I think of you on my bed,
  and meditate on you in the watches of the night;
for you have been my help,
  and in the shadow of your wings I sing for joy.
My soul clings to you;
  your right hand upholds me.

Psalm 63:1–8

So he came to a Samaritan city called Sychar, near the plot of ground that Jacob had given to his son Joseph. Jacob's well was there, and Jesus, tired out by his journey, was sitting by the well. It was about noon.

A Samaritan woman came to draw water, and Jesus said to her, "Give me a drink." (His disciples had gone to the city to buy food.) The Samaritan woman said to him, "How is it that you, a Jew, ask a drink of me, a woman of Samaria?" (Jews do not share things in common with Samaritans.) Jesus answered her, "If you knew the gift of God, and who it is that is saying to you, 'Give me a drink,' you would have asked him, and he would have given you living water." . . . The woman said to him, "I know that Messiah is coming" (who is called Christ). "When he comes, he will proclaim all things to us." Jesus said to her, "I am he, the one who is speaking to you."

Just then his disciples came. They were astonished that he was speaking with a woman, but no one said, "What do you want?" or, "Why are you speaking with her?" Then the woman left her water jar and went back to the city. She said to the people, "Come and see a man who told me everything I have ever done! He cannot be the Messiah, can he?" They left the city and were on their way to him.

John 4:5–10, 25–30

Look to the Sky

In her book *The Quotidian Mysteries*, Kathleen Norris invites people to find the sacred in ordinary things—like seeing a sink full of dirty dishes as a holy invitation to play.[10] While I struggle with living out this invitation in dishwashing, I embrace it fully when I am watering my garden; it is not at all uncommon on a really hot day for me to stick my head under the sprayer for a few moments while watering. I love water. I love swimming, I love kayaking, I love scuba diving. I love playing in water. I even love listening to the sounds of rainfall as "white noise" through my headphones.

The life of the gardener necessitates a constant watch on the weather, especially rain. I need to know if it rained last night while I was sleeping, and if so, how much. I keep an eye on the forecast, the sky, and the moisture in the soil of the garden beds. When my peace lily plant is thirsty, it begins to droop. Within an hour or so of watering it, it perks right back up. Unfortunately, most of the food we grow doesn't communicate as clearly as my peace lily. Tomato plants do not convey their feelings so readily; I must be far more vigilant in monitoring their conditions.

Modern city and suburban culture has detached us from weather in some fascinating ways. One year on my father's birthday, my sister and I arranged to spend the day with him at a Kansas City Royals baseball game, one of our favorite family activities. As we sat in the stands, somewhere around the third or fourth inning, a light mist began to fall. My sister and I, like many people around us, quickly whipped out our cell phones to look at the cloud formations in the weather forecasts. As the rain began to fall harder, I gave up and put my phone away. As my clothes were already completely soaked, I figured it didn't really matter; at that point, it would stop raining when it stopped raining. But my sister sat with her phone and kept insisting, "It wasn't supposed to rain today! I checked a million times. Look at this map! The rain isn't even over us!" Laughing, I held up my hands and said, "Well, I guess no one informed the sky of your cell phone's weather forecast!" As I have considered that day, I have often wondered: How often do we sit in the pouring rain, insisting it can't be raining, simply because technology tells us otherwise?

I once heard of a young lady "from the big city" who stopped at a gas station in a rural area. It was pouring down rain that day, and she was very unhappy about traveling in the rain. She voiced her frustration loudly near the coffee booths where several locals were sitting. They all sat and shook their heads as she complained; they didn't share her frustration at all. Rather, the farm community had been rejoicing all day because the rain marked the end of a long and painful drought. For farmers, what happens with the weather is a matter of their professional well-being. However, for most suburban and city dwellers—a majority of American citizens—the connection between nature and our food sources is almost completely invisible, so much so that things like rain are mere traveling barriers or "good for the lawn."

Thirst

Life as we know it requires water to survive. Some scientists have theorized there may be life on other planets that can exist without water, but humans haven't discovered any of those life-forms yet.

Prior to some recent water-safety crises, such as the one in Flint, Michigan, most people in the United States took access to clean water for granted. Water comes out of a tap when I turn it on—no big deal. But this is part of the problem. For far too long, we have taken our water sources for granted. We have not given them the respect they deserve. We have allowed companies to pour endless substances into our waterways, and we do not consider what is washing away from farms into the water system. During the Standing Rock protests, many Native Americans repeatedly introduced America to the Lakota saying "Water is life."

In most hospice scenarios, there comes a time when the patients can no longer consume liquids; most often they no longer have the energy or consciousness required to swallow. But the inability to swallow in no way abates the body's need for liquid. Without adequate attention, a patient's lips and mouth will start to crack from being so dry. Hospice care offers some relief to this common problem. First, some sort of balm is applied to the lips of the dying person. Second, there are these fabulous tiny sponges on sticks (sometimes they are flavored and scented like peppermint) that a medical attendant or family member can dip into water and then use to moisten the mouth and lips of the patient.

As a pastor, I have been present at many deathbeds. I have seen many dying people respond, for the first time in hours or even days, when they receive this gift of their mouth being moistened with the sponge. Once in a while, a particularly stubborn individual will even clamp down on the sponge in the first voluntary movement the family has seen in some time. Even in the throes of death, our bodies cry out for water.

The psalmist addresses thirst in a poetic manner, but rather than referring to thirst for water, the psalmist refers to thirsting for God. I suspect few Christians have ever thirsted for God the way mortal bodies thirst for water. When a person (or animal) has been deprived of water and food for days on end, what is the first thing they will choose—food or water? Inevitably, it is water, and not just for the practical reason that until thirst is quenched, food will be hard to choke down a dry throat. The psalmist longs for God in this urgent and desperate way, and we are called to do the same.

At the Well

In our New Testament text for this week, we see the woman at the well, who is a fascinating character. While a million assumptions have been made about her in the past two thousand years, we do know a few key facts about this unnamed woman. The first is that in Jesus' time, women were not considered fully human. In both Jesus' era and in our own, many men consider being called a feminine name or slur to be the ultimate insult. This stems from a deeply held and lasting belief that being female is something of which one ought to be ashamed. Jesus was violating social norms by speaking to a woman when she did not have a male relative present.

Secondly, the woman was a Samaritan. Samaritans branched off from Jews during the time when the Israelites were divided into northern and southern kingdoms. The southern kingdom (Judah) contained Jerusalem, the only place the descendants of Abraham and Sarah could rightly worship Yahweh. So the king and leaders of the northern kingdom (Israel) established new places to worship so that their people would have no reason to enter the southern kingdom. The northern people—who believed a person could worship Yahweh somewhere other than Jerusalem—became known as Samaritans, and despite the political and theological split being seven hundred years old by Jesus' time, the Jewish people still thought so little of the apostate Samaritans that they avoided even speaking to them. This is part of the reason why when the Samaritan turns out to be the hero in the parable of the Good Samaritan, the message is a scandal—a "good Samaritan" would have been considered a complete oxymoron in Jesus' time.

So when Jesus, a good Jewish man, asks a Samaritan woman for a drink of water, it is shocking and disturbing to those who later hear the story. One can almost hear the gasp of the astonished crowd: "How could he associate with people like her?" Throughout his life and teaching, Jesus repeatedly disregards social norms and stereotypes. He is not offering the woman at the well a cup of water, but the refreshment of everlasting life.

Despite his divine disregard for so many human things, the human part of Jesus is most likely exhausted and thirsty from the journey. Examples of the importance of water are abundant throughout

Scripture; since most of the biblical narrative takes place in the desert, it makes sense that a people living in an arid region would be so concerned with water. But when we look at water's place throughout the narratives of human culture, the thread runs deep through a variety of cultures, religions, and mythologies. Human beings have long incorporated this fundamental necessity of life into our daily rituals, be they religious or social habits. In Christianity, water becomes the fundamental focus in baptism—in the water that brings everlasting life—and is the same water that means the woman at the well will never be thirsty again.

By Water and the Spirit

I baptized a lot of children in my first few years in ministry. In my first year out of seminary, most of the baptisms were heartbreaking events; I was serving as a hospital chaplain, and most of the babies I baptized were in crisis situations. I baptized the tiniest souls, sometimes weighing little more than one pound. I adjusted the baptismal liturgy normally used in the United Methodist tradition because I could not in good conscience ask a parent of a child everyone knew had at most a few days to live, "Will you nurture this child in Christ's holy Church, that by your teaching and example she may be guided to accept God's grace for herself, to profess her faith openly, and to lead a Christian life?" Those children were not going to grow up. While I was honored to be a part of these sacred moments, they were heartbreaking.

When I was appointed as the associate pastor to a large church with lots of young families, I was incredibly excited to be baptizing healthy children for the first time. Baptism days were my favorite Sundays by far. I had a practice of meeting with the family prior to the service so that I could get acquainted with the child being baptized. Interestingly, most families waited until their children were old enough to hold up their own heads, so part of the preparation on the day of the service was showing the children the baptismal font. Almost every baby old enough to do so would reach out and want to play in the water. I encouraged this, so much so that I frequently had a child trying to squirm out of my arms to play in the baptismal font during the service. I loved this image of a child reaching for the baptismal waters, happily splashing in them. Chubby hands banged on the water, and joyous laughter rang out as water splashed everywhere. I was happily drenched more than once. I had a few parents who were concerned when their little one wanted to play in the baptismal font, thinking it might be disrespectful or sacrilegious, but I always assured them that Jesus would definitely have approved. I firmly believe Jesus would have laughed and joined in the fun.

The baptismal liturgy in my own United Methodist tradition begins with these words: "Through the Sacrament of Baptism we are initiated into Christ's holy Church. We are incorporated into God's mighty acts of salvation and given new birth through water and the Spirit. All this is God's gift, offered to us without price."[11] The liturgy goes on to affirm many of the times God has worked through water: in creation, in saving Noah and his family from the flood, in parting the Red Sea as the Hebrew people escaped slavery in Egypt, and through the waters that gave Jesus life while he was still in Mary's womb. God's relationship with water seems almost as intertwined as our own.

Indeed, our relationship with water goes far beyond enjoyment and recreation. Water is so powerful that it can cut through solid rock, given enough time. And while all life requires water for physical survival, our spiritual survival depends on the grace offered through the baptismal waters. While water blessed for baptism is still just water, it also becomes something more—a force containing the cleansing promise of God's redemption and grace. Without water, there is no life—in both the physical and the spiritual realms.

QUESTIONS FOR REFLECTION AND DISCUSSION

1. Discuss your own memories of water—a time when you were thirsty, a childhood memory of swimming or of running through sprinklers, or even the first time you saw the ocean. How can water be a source of relief and joy?
2. How does city/suburban life separate people from the patterns of precipitation? How might we reframe our conversations about weather in terms of what our local food producers need? Why might this matter?

3. The psalmist describes "thirsting for God." How have you thirsted for God? Have you experienced times of drought in your spiritual life when you longed for God? What were those experiences like?
4. Who might be the "Samaritans" of our time? What groups of people are excluded or outcast in our culture? How do we respond as Jesus and interact with those communities with a spirit of "living water"? How do we work for justice with these populations?
5. Have you ever failed at growing a plant because you forgot to water it? What happened to the plant as it died? What did it look like? How might this mirror what happens to our souls without the living water of which Jesus speaks?
6. How does your tradition understand the significance of the baptismal waters? How do you understand being washed clean and becoming a new creation through baptism?

DAILY REFLECTIONS

Monday

All life as we know it requires water to survive. If you have someplace you can go to be near a body of water this week (lake, creek, ocean, etc.), take advantage of the opportunity and contemplate the miracle of water in God's creation.

Tuesday

Do you have running water in your home? If so, take some time today to be thankful for access to clean water. By even the most conservative estimates, billions of people around the world do not have consistent access to clean water. In the United States, we often take such a basic part of life for granted. Consider researching some groups that are trying to provide clean water around the world. (One such fantastic group is Well Aware.) How is water a justice issue in this context? How are we as God's people called to act in the face of such injustice?

Wednesday

In Matthew 5:45, Jesus says that God makes the "sun rise on the evil and on the good, and sends rain on the righteous and on the unrighteous." In times of flood, rain seems like an unprovoked curse upon the righteous. In times of drought, rain seems like an unwarranted blessing for the unrighteous. What do we do with this truth Jesus speaks? What truth might it speak into your life today?

Thursday

Lectio Divina ("divine reading" in Latin) is an ancient Christian practice for communing with Scripture. The focus of Lectio Divina is not theological study; rather, it is a spiritual practice to help an individual grow closer to God. Lectio Divina has four steps: read, meditate, pray, and contemplate. Take some time to practice Lectio Divina with Psalm 63 today by reading the text and then meditating on, praying over, and contemplating it. Set a specific number of minutes for yourself to engage with the text in each of these four separate ways. (For instance, if you decide on three minutes per step, you will spend a total of twelve minutes on today's devotional.)

Friday

In her book *The Quotidian Mysteries*, Kathleen Norris states that a sink full of dirty dishes is really God offering us an invitation to play. Today, find time to play in water, whether it is in a sink full of dishes, a bath, or a shower; you may even want to celebrate childhood with some water guns. Rediscover just how much fun creation can be; God will be rejoicing and laughing right beside you.

Saturday

Today, consider your baptism. Look up the baptismal covenant for your tradition. What are the promises that you made or that were made on your behalf? What parts of the baptismal ritual in your tradition speak to you most clearly today? If you have never been baptized, speak with a pastor or friend about what the promise of baptism means. Today, when you shower, bathe, or wash your hands, reflect on the baptismal waters.

Fourth Sunday of Lent

LIGHT

1 Samuel 16:1–13; John 3:14–21

The LORD said to Samuel, "How long will you grieve over Saul? I have rejected him from being king over Israel. . . . I will send you to Jesse the Bethlehemite, for I have provided for myself a king among his sons." . . .

When they came, he looked on Eliab and thought, "Surely the LORD's anointed is now before the LORD." But the LORD said to Samuel, "Do not look on his appearance or on the height of his stature, because I have rejected him; for the LORD does not see as mortals see; they look on the outward appearance, but the LORD looks on the heart." . . . Jesse made seven of his sons pass before Samuel, and Samuel said to Jesse, "The LORD has not chosen any of these." Samuel said to Jesse, "Are all your sons here?" And he said, "There remains yet the youngest, but he is keeping the sheep." And Samuel said to Jesse, "Send and bring him; for we will not sit down until he comes here." He sent and brought him in. Now he was ruddy, and had beautiful eyes, and was handsome. The LORD said, "Rise and anoint him; for this is the one." Then Samuel took the horn of oil, and anointed him in the presence of his brothers; and the spirit of the LORD came mightily upon David from that day forward.

1 Samuel 16:1, 6–7, 10–13a

"Indeed, God did not send the Son into the world to condemn the world, but in order that the world might be saved through him. Those who believe in him are not condemned; but those who do not believe are condemned already, because they

> have not believed in the name of the only Son of God. And this is the judgment, that the light has come into the world, and people loved darkness rather than light because their deeds were evil. For all who do evil hate the light and do not come to the light, so that their deeds may not be exposed. But those who do what is true come to the light, so that it may be clearly seen that their deeds have been done in God."
>
> John 3:17–21

Halfway Out of the Dark

Once during my ministry the Fourth Sunday of Lent happened to fall on the same Sunday as the beginning of daylight savings time. That doesn't happen very often, but it seemed fitting that on the Sunday we thought about light in worship, we were given an extra hour of it. The timing of Easter is based on the spring equinox, equinox being the solar midpoint between the shortest (winter solstice) and longest (summer solstice) days of the year in the northern hemisphere. In other words, Easter falls around the time of year when there begin to be more hours of daylight than of darkness—regardless of the time change. By contrast, Christmas always falls a few days from the winter solstice—the darkest day of the year. After that, it can only get lighter.

As an avid fan of the television show *Dr. Who*, I eagerly await the release of the Christmas special each year. In one such episode, "A Christmas Carol," the show begins with a voice-over:

> On every world, wherever people are in the deepest part of the winter, at the exact midpoint everybody stops, and turns, and hugs as if to say, "Well done. Well done, everyone! We're halfway out of the dark." Back on Earth, we called this Christmas, or the winter solstice.[12]

I love this quote, and I think about it every year at Christmas. Like most people, I love long days full of sunlight, and the short, cold days of winter can get me down. The hardest part of the year for me is when the Christmas tree comes down, when the Christmas decorations and lights have been put away, and there are still several months of cold and dark to endure.

Human beings, like most diurnal creatures, are drawn to the light. (Diurnal is the opposite of nocturnal.) Our bodies are not primed for darkness in the way that those of many other creatures are; we are blind in complete darkness. Because most human beings rely so heavily on our sense of sight for navigating the world, it makes sense that cultures across the world have themes of being afraid of the dark; we frighten one another with tales of things that "go bump in the night." What we can see is always less terrifying than what we can imagine lurking somewhere, invisible. I find psychological thrillers more frightening than horror movies; I can imagine far scarier things than any director can put on screen.

During the 1990s there was a show on Nickelodeon called *Are You Afraid of the Dark?* (The show's popularity sparked a reboot in 2019 for nostalgic millennials.) In the show, a group of teenagers called "the Midnight Society" gathered around a campfire to tell scary stories to one another. As a child I kept watching the show, even though at the end of each episode, the answer to the show's title question, "Are you afraid of the dark?" was a resounding "I am now!" I confess I slept with the bedside lamp on more nights than not when I had watched the show.

Even in adulthood, whenever the power goes out, I am consistently amazed by the silence and the dark. We don't give a lot of consideration to the buzzing around us all the time—the air conditioner, the heater, a fan, the television, the radio. The silence is almost deafening when the power goes out, even though we barely notice the white noise around us. Similarly, I forget just how dark my house can be without the shine of digital clocks, the flashing lights of power cords, and the glow of computer screens.

When I was ten years old, I went to camp for the first time. Even though I had spent quite a bit of time in rural areas visiting my grandparents during childhood, their homes, with bright lights on the porch, did not prepare me for the remote woods of camp. At camp, I had my first real taste of darkness. And even at the age of ten, it was terrifying. It was the sort of darkness where you wave your hand in front of your face and can't see it; it was the sort of darkness where you are not sure if you can still see. I woke up each morning a little embarrassed by how tightly I had clutched my flashlight the night before.

With the exception of cave-dwelling organisms, light is essential to most life as we know it. Even deep-sea creatures feed on the detritus that floats down from the zones where there is light. If I plant seed potatoes in the best soil, water them every day, and tend to them in all the ways I should but keep them in a dark closet, you know what will happen to them? They will rot. Nothing will grow.

Light is necessary in the life of the garden, and the amount of sunlight a plant receives matters significantly. Various levels of light are needed to make different plants happy, and it's important to keep this in mind when planting flowers or shrubbery. Certain flowers will wither and die if they are in "full sun," which means they are exposed to the sun all day long. Some flowers thrive in "partial sun," meaning they are in the shade about half the day. Other plants, like peace lilies, will wilt and die in direct sunlight. However, the majority of foods we eat grow best in full sun (one of the major exceptions in the human diet being mushrooms, which prefer full shade). In the summer months in the northern hemisphere, this can mean an incredibly large amount of time in the sun. Access to sunlight makes a significant difference in where a garden can be successful, based on the location of surrounding buildings and trees. While hardy plants, such as herbs, might do all right without access to full sun, a tomato plant is unlikely to thrive in such conditions.

While the Old Testament passage for this week is largely concerned with seeing, human sight requires light. Yahweh opens Samuel's eyes to which one of Jesse's sons is right to become the next king of Israel. It is as though God turns on a light so that Samuel can properly see that the least likely of Jesse's sons is the right choice.

God Turns on a Light

From the time Joshua led the Hebrew people across the Jordan, through the ages of the judges of Israel, the people of Israel had insisted they needed a king. Yahweh told them time and time again that a king was a bad idea. And yet like teenagers who insist they need whatever brand or item makes a young person "cool" at a given moment, the Israelites saw that all the nations around them had kings. The people wanted what everyone else around them had.

Yahweh finally gives the people what they think they want. Saul is anointed the first king of Israel. True to all the prophecies that warned of the dangers of a king, Saul turns out to be a less-than-desirable king. Most terrifying to Saul's subjects, his mind begins to sink into a state of chaotic paranoia. It is in this setting, with a psychologically unstable king on the throne, that the prophet Samuel is called by Yahweh to anoint a new king of Israel. Yahweh tells Samuel outright, "I have rejected [Saul] from being king over Israel" (1 Sam. 16:1).

Samuel is not happy about this assignment—hence his response: "How can I go? If Saul hears of it, he will kill me" (16:2). He is going behind the king's back to declare a new king—one who is not of Saul's bloodline. Despite Saul's mental and emotional descent into paranoia, Saul would be within his rights and quite justified in declaring Samuel's act of naming a new king what it is: treason. Samuel knows this action is a capital offense.

When Samuel meets Jesse, he tells him to gather together his sons. In ancient Israel, birth order mattered; it mattered a lot. The firstborn son was the rightful heir of his father. A son far down in the birth order, like David, would have inherited next to nothing from his father. It is not the least bit surprising that Jesse does not bother calling in his youngest son from the field. Kings in this time period went into war with their troops; how could a little boy like David lead an entire army? He was not the right choice for the lofty position of king. As Samuel observes Jesse's sons lined up from eldest to youngest, he moves down the line thinking, "Yes, this is a fine young man—he must be the one," only to be thwarted by God until he arrives at the least likely choice. God opens Samuel's eyes to God's will—despite the selection of David going against all social structures and beliefs of the time. The light of God's truth illuminates the darkness.

The Light of the World

The Gospel of John spends a lot of time considering light. Indeed, rather than the Christmas story we find in the Gospels of Matthew and Luke, John begins with a discourse on Jesus being "the Word": "What has come into being in him was life, and the life was the light of all people. The light shines in the darkness, and the darkness did not overcome it" (John 1:3b–5). In John 8:12, Jesus speaks these words: "I am the light of the world. Whoever follows me will never walk in darkness but will have the light of life."

I grow weary when people tell me they take Scripture literally. I find this statement suspect; there are plenty of places where one verse is the complete opposite of another verse. Furthermore, there are so many parts of Scripture in which the writer clearly does not intend to be interpreted literally, passages that include metaphor, allegory, and even poetry. But perhaps this metaphor of Jesus as light in the Gospel of John is one of the best examples. Does Jesus bring metaphorical light to my life? Absolutely. But Jesus makes one heck of a lousy flashlight when my power goes out.

The theme of light as good and dark as bad is a prevalent archetype throughout Western culture, from religious themes to pop culture. (Any *Star Wars* fan worth their salt can tell you why giving in to the Dark Side of the Force is a very bad thing.) This is largely because what takes place in the light can be seen—so light is associated with honesty, transparency, openness, and the good. What takes place in the dark cannot be seen, so it is associated with lies, secrecy, stealth, and evil.

It should be noted that the light versus dark dichotomy has been used as a tool in systemic racism, especially to justify assigning more humanity to people with light skin as opposed to those with dark skin. This justification for racism has even been used in the history of the church. Despite the modern misuse of this narrative, the writers of the Gospels were referring not to skin color but to a day-versus-night separation.

Today's passage from John casts judgment on the world—that people "loved darkness rather than light because their deeds are evil." Perhaps we should also cast judgment, not on others but on ourselves. In Alcoholics Anonymous, the fourth step in the twelve-step program is to do a "fearless moral inventory." Part of the reason for this is that we must accept the things we have done wrong to begin to move past them toward change. I suspect all Christians would both benefit from and be intimidated by an annual "fearless moral inventory"—and isn't this the essence of Lent? We are called to turn on the light in the dark corners of our lives we attempt to hide from God, others, and ourselves.

For generations, pastors were taught to hide the ugly parts of themselves in preaching. There was a common belief that revealing flaws from the pulpit would inherently cause a loss of pastoral authority. But in recent years, many pastors have begun to bring to light the parts of their lives in which they have struggled, questioned, or doubted. Some of the most powerful words we can hear from another person are "I've been through something similar. You are not alone." I have lost track of the number of people who have admitted to me, laden with shame and secrecy, that they are taking an antidepressant or antianxiety medication. I usually follow up their confession by saying, "Thank you for trusting me. I also take an antidepressant every morning." I have often witnessed an immediate shift in body language with such individuals, as though they suddenly realize, "Hey, if my pastor needs an antidepressant, maybe it's okay that I couldn't pray away my depression!"

It is no wonder that with generations of spiritual leaders believing they must keep their every flaw hidden in the dark, so many Christians feel they cannot bring their own flaws into the light. There are a multitude of times when, if only we could share the parts of our lives we find shameful or embarrassing, we might find healing. I once had three mothers in one small congregation who were all keeping the secret that each of them had a son in prison. They each shared this in close confidence with me. I tried to find a way to connect these women, but none of them wanted to risk sharing the information with other church members, even ones who were in a similar situation. I could only imagine how they might have benefited from one another's experiences and company if there had been more openness. I believe the old cliché is true: a burden shared is a burden lightened. Just as seeds brought out of the dark have an opportunity to grow, we have an opportunity to grow when we bring our full selves into the light of Christ.

QUESTIONS FOR REFLECTION AND DISCUSSION

1. Have you ever had a "lightbulb" moment? Has God ever opened your eyes to a new truth or insight? Describe what that was like.

2. Are there times when you crave sunlight? When do you feel this most strongly?
3. When have you experienced complete darkness? What is that like? Were you afraid? Why do we tell scary stories in the dark to heighten their fright factor? What does darkness add to a scary story or scary movie?
4. What is meant by "spiritual sight" in Samuel's story? How might spiritual sight be useful in the Christian life? How might the Holy Spirit work through spiritual sight?
5. Jesus says, "For all who do evil hate the light and do not come to the light, so that their deeds may not be exposed" (John 3:20). How does this basic truth play out in human society, both literally and metaphorically?
6. What would a "fearless moral inventory" look like for you? How might light be shed on dark corners of your own life?

DAILY REFLECTIONS

Monday

There is an instinctual fear of the dark in human beings. Why do you think this is? Why are we drawn to light? Why are God and the good so frequently associated with the light of day, whereas evil is associated with the darkness of night?

Tuesday

This evening after nightfall, find a dark room and give yourself permission to play with a flashlight. Did you ever play with a flashlight as a child? Many of my childhood memories of power outages are positive ones, because it meant we got to play with the flashlights. What memories do you have involving flashlights? What does it mean when Jesus says, "I am the light of the world?" How can Christ light up our lives in the way the flashlight lights up the room?

Wednesday

When seedlings are started under a grow light, they need to be hardened before they can be planted out in the garden. This means setting them out in the sun for a little longer each day before finally transplanting them into their permanent outdoor homes. While the grow light simulates the sun, it is no match for the intensity of the sun's rays, and so a plant that has not been hardened will often wither and die. Consider your spiritual journey. Have there been times when you have been hardened by life and circumstances only to be better prepared for a greater challenge that was yet to come? How have those difficult times shaped your understanding of the Divine?

Thursday

While working on this book, I slipped on a patch of ice and fell, hitting my head. This resulted in a serious concussion; I lost the ability to speak for several minutes and lost my short-term memory for several hours. Although both came back that day, full recovery from the concussion took many weeks. For months I was extremely sensitive to certain types of light and had trouble with the rapid shifts of sunlight and shadows when riding in a car. I suddenly became aware and sensitive to light and shadow in ways I had never been before. It may not have been the result of a brain injury, but have you ever paid attention to the play of light and shadow? What has that experience been like? What drew your attention to the light or shadow?

Friday

As a person with very fair skin, I underestimated the sun a few times in my formative years (those years of learning where there is no longer a parent hovering over one's shoulder). The result of my underestimation was always the same: a painful sunburn. Although the result is not always as painful, I have found that we can underestimate God. While we believe in God's power theoretically, sometimes we forget to turn to God in times of crisis. How do you make sure you turn to God first in your daily life?

Saturday

If the seeds you planted at the beginning of the series have not yet sprouted, they most likely will not. Replant some seeds if you have yet to see sprouts. If you have seen sprouts, what has it been like watching them grow? How has it influenced your understanding of "a time to grow"?

Fifth Sunday of Lent

RESTORATION

Ezekiel 37:1–14; John 11:1–45

The hand of the LORD came upon me, and he brought me out by the spirit of the LORD and set me down in the middle of a valley; it was full of bones. He led me all around them; there were very many lying in the valley, and they were very dry. He said to me, "Mortal, can these bones live?" I answered, "O Lord GOD, you know." Then he said to me, "Prophesy to these bones, and say to them: O dry bones, hear the word of the LORD." . . .

So I prophesied as I had been commanded; and as I prophesied, suddenly there was a noise, a rattling, and the bones came together, bone to its bone. I looked, and there were sinews on them, and flesh had come upon them, and skin had covered them; but there was no breath in them. Then he said to me, "Prophesy to the breath, prophesy, mortal, and say to the breath: Thus says the Lord GOD: Come from the four winds, O breath, and breathe upon these slain, that they may live." I prophesied as he commanded me, and the breath came into them, and they lived, and stood on their feet, a vast multitude.

Then he said to me, "Mortal, these bones are the whole house of Israel. They say, 'Our bones are dried up, and our hope is lost; we are cut off completely.' Therefore prophesy, and say to them, Thus says the Lord GOD: I am going to open your graves, and bring you up from your graves, O my people; and I will bring you back to the land of Israel. And you shall know that I am the LORD, when I open your graves, and bring you up from your graves, O my people. I will put my spirit within you, and you shall live, and I will place you on your own soil; then you shall know that I, the LORD, have spoken and will act, says the LORD."

Ezekiel 37:1–4, 7–14

When Jesus arrived, he found that Lazarus had already been in the tomb four days. Now Bethany was near Jerusalem, some two miles away, and many of the Jews had come to Martha and Mary to console them about their brother. When Martha heard that Jesus was coming, she went and met him, while Mary stayed at home. Martha said to Jesus, "Lord, if you had been here, my brother would not have died. But even now I know that God will give you whatever you ask of him." . . .

He said, "Where have you laid him?" They said to him, "Lord, come and see." Jesus began to weep. So the Jews said, "See how he loved him!" But some of them said, "Could not he who opened the eyes of the blind man have kept this man from dying?"

Then Jesus, again greatly disturbed, came to the tomb. It was a cave, and a stone was lying against it. Jesus said, "Take away the stone." Martha, the sister of the dead man, said to him, "Lord, already there is a stench because he has been dead four days." Jesus said to her, "Did I not tell you that if you believed, you would see the glory of God?" So they took away the stone. And Jesus looked upward and said, "Father, I thank you for having heard me. I knew that you always hear me, but I have said this for the sake of the crowd standing here, so that they may believe that you sent me." When he had said this, he cried with a loud voice, "Lazarus, come out!" The dead man came out, his hands and feet bound with strips of cloth, and his face wrapped in a cloth. Jesus said to them, "Unbind him, and let him go."

John 11:17–22, 34–44

Blueberry Thief

A vendor at our local farmers market had the most beautiful blueberry bushes for sale for several seasons. My husband and I decided to purchase a few, even though we had no experience growing blueberries. We spoke with the vendor extensively before our purchase and made sure we were ready to bring our blueberry bushes home. We knew how to prepare the earth for the transplant into our garden, how to water the bushes throughout the season, and even what fertilizer the bushes would need when they stopped producing fruit each summer.

We followed all the vendor's instructions and had a delicious—if tiny—crop of blueberries that first summer. One day, in the middle of the following winter, I went out the back door to check on something and was met with a horrible sight—our blueberry bushes were gone! It looked as though they had been chopped down, right where they emerged from the earth. There was not a trace of the bushes left in our entire yard. But who would do such a thing? Who would bother to enter our fenced backyard, chop down both bushes, and then carry the useless branches away with them?

After a little research, we quickly learned that rabbits will sometimes eat even the woody parts of blueberry bushes in the winter. Apparently our blueberry bushes had been consumed by some mischievous and hungry bunnies.

As things warmed up that spring, we devised a plan to protect future blueberry bushes from rabbits. Before purchasing two new bushes at the farmers market, I went out to remove the rabbit-eaten stumps and prepare the space for new bushes. On the first stump, I pulled out what was left of the roots with minimal effort. But the stump of the second blueberry bush would not yield. I dug around the remaining roots to get a good grip, but no matter how hard I pulled, the stump refused to budge. My husband also gave it a try when he arrived home, but to no avail.

We finally decided to leave it alone and see if the stump would grow. While we did not have blueberries that summer, by the end of the summer the bush had grown back to the size it had been when we put it in the earth. The stump sent out shoots, and more shoots, and a year later we were harvesting blueberries once more.

Like plants that have voluntarily been restored, Christians center the resurrection at the heart of our story of the good news of Jesus Christ. If we could tell a person only one story from

Scripture to summarize the Christian faith, wouldn't it be the story of resurrection?

But sometimes I wonder—if we really believe in resurrection, why are we so afraid of death? We preach and teach about resurrection constantly, but I have often seen people cling desperately to scraps of life. When all that is left is a shell, all that is left is dry bones, sometimes resurrection is the only viable restoration. Sometimes we need to make the gamble that we haven't just been prattling on about nothing for all these years. How very foolish, yet how very human, to love what is mortal.

Ruach

There is a spark of life in all creatures that cannot be replicated, duplicated, or synthesized. That spark of life is never more apparent than when one is in the room with someone who has just died. There is a moment when the person is alive, and then there is an ineffable essence that suddenly is no more. This spark is the *ruach*, the breath of life, the spark of what keeps us alive; it is the miracle of God within us.

The passage from Ezekiel contains incredibly vivid imagery. Ezekiel's prophetic ministry took place at a time when the people of Israel were in exile in Babylon. The aforementioned southern kingdom, Judah, was conquered by the Babylonians around 587 BCE. (The northern kingdom, Israel, had fallen to the Assyrians about 130 years earlier.) The fall of Judah also meant the fall of Jerusalem, which you'll recall was considered the only proper place for Yahweh to be worshiped. The destruction and conquering of Judah was deeply troubling to the people—as is any conquest of one's homeland. But the destruction and desecration of the temple in Jerusalem inflicted spiritual damage that is difficult for those of us in the twenty-first century to understand.

In the region surrounding ancient Israel, there were theological premises that were universal to the region, despite differences in faith among various cultures. One such universally accepted theological premise maintained that a conquering nation had defeated the god or gods of the conquered. The people of Judah had, much like the people of Israel before them, believed that Yahweh would protect them because they were Yahweh's people. Thus, logically, watching their own army be conquered meant either that Yahweh had abandoned them, the gods of Babylon were stronger than Yahweh, or a combination of the two.

Adding insult to injury, the best, brightest, and most skilled inhabitants of Judah were then captured and taken to Babylon. It was a common strategy, both brilliant and effective, of conquering nations at that time in history. When one nation conquered another to hold as a province, the victor would ship the residents most capable of leading a rebellion to the heart of its own empire. It was an excellent way to maintain newly acquired territory and to prevent uprisings among provinces.

Ezekiel prophesied to the exiled people of Judah, who were in a state of political, geographical, and spiritual exile. They were defeated and lost; Ezekiel's vision offered hope to a people who had long lived without hope. His vision intended to plant the seeds of hope in the hearts of those who heard it.

In Ezekiel's vision, he sees the battlefield on which the Judean army had been slaughtered. Indeed, the bones of which he speaks are all that remains of the bodies of fallen Judean soldiers. Understanding Ezekiel's context is critical when contemplating the weight of God's question: "Can these bones live?" It's not just about the resurrection of dry bones—it's about the resurrection of God's people. God is asking a far more critical question: "Can Israel live again?"

Ezekiel responds wisely, "Only you know, O Lord." And before Ezekiel's eyes, the bones begin to come together, the sinews begin to form, organs and muscles reappear and then are covered with flesh. Finally, standing before Ezekiel, is an army restored to life. But they are not yet fully alive until God breathes into them the "breath of life."

The English translation "breath" is somewhat insufficient for explaining the weight of this passage. This is not the fault of the translators but is simply the fact that there is no word in English for the Hebrew concept contained in the word *ruach*. The *ruach* is not just breath—this is not simply a divine form of CPR. The word can also mean mind, breath, wind, or spirit, as seen in the creation story in the second chapter of Genesis. God forms the human beings out of the dust of the earth, but they are not fully alive until God breathes into them the *ruach*, or the "breath of life."

This "breath of life" is the same life that fills the body of Lazarus when Jesus raises him from the dead. Lazarus is revived, but his body will still die again.

Resurrection

Just before my nineteenth birthday, I had to have surgery around my shoulder area. When the surgery was over and I was in recovery, my parents were allowed to come back and see me. As they stood by my bed, I suddenly had difficulty breathing. Asthmatic since the age of seven, I asked for my inhaler, my lifelong response to shortness of breath, but the inhaler made no difference. Soon breathing became more and more difficult. Later we learned that my lung cavity had been nicked during surgery, a common complication with the procedure, resulting in the collapse of my right lung.

I remember my parents standing over me, repeatedly reminding me to breathe as my body slowly succumbed to exhaustion. I felt in my abdomen that my body was giving up, and I strangely remember recognizing the oncoming of death for what it was. While heartbroken that my life had come to an end, I didn't think death was so bad. Likely as a result of the lack of oxygen, I began to feel very peaceful.

And then a doctor slid a scalpel between my ribs, underneath my arm. The medical staff inserted a chest tube that would allow my lung to reinflate while simultaneously sucking any fluid out of my lung. It was the most painful moment of my life. In all honesty, the thought most prevalent in that moment was "Why didn't you let me die? Death wouldn't be so bad. But this? This is hell!" The next twenty-four hours were the most painful I have ever endured. Every breath felt like I was being stabbed in the side. These many years later, I am grateful to that doctor for saving my life, but in that moment I was angry, resentful, and even hateful.

Whenever I read the story of Lazarus, I cannot help but remember that day. Lazarus had been dead for several days. Jews of that time believed that all souls descended into Sheol. While many Christian traditions believe the dead go to a place of eternal punishment (hell) or eternal reward (heaven), Sheol is neither of those things. It is simply the realm of the dead. Jewish people of the time would have believed that Lazarus's soul had already descended into Sheol. Lazarus was wrapped in cloth and entombed with his family members who had preceded him in death. The family tomb surely smelled terrible, despite all the spices and scents used in preparation of the body. Upon his resurrection, Lazarus went from the peace of death into the rank smell of rotting flesh with his face completely wrapped in fabric. While I am certain Lazarus was eventually grateful to Jesus, I suspect, upon reflection, that Lazarus was less than grateful in those first few moments.

As a pastor, I am around death a lot—it comes with the job. I have sat at many bedsides waiting for a parishioner or patient to die, and I have had the privilege of being in the room on many occasions when people have taken their final breaths. There is nothing like a lifeless body to convince me of the significance of the *ruach* in animating our very being. There is a spark of life that science cannot fully understand or describe, but that spark of life is everything. Without it, we are but dust.

QUESTIONS FOR REFLECTION AND DISCUSSION

1. Have you ever had a resurrection moment with a plant, pet, or even a loved one? Describe the experience.
2. What can different forms of restoration look like? For individuals? For communities? For churches?
3. What do we learn about God's relationship with humankind in the Ezekiel passage? What might this teach us about how God relates to us?
4. What is the meaning of *ruach*? How might *ruach* relate to the work of the Holy Spirit? What is the significance of life requiring *ruach* to exist?
5. What does the restoration of Lazarus's life mean for him? For his sisters? What would it mean for you to go from death to life?
6. What is the significance of "new life" in resurrection? If your tradition has a baptismal liturgy, read over this liturgy again. If

it does not, consider your own baptism or baptisms you have witnessed. How do you understand the role of new life in the baptismal covenant?

DAILY REFLECTIONS

Monday

Restoration can mean many things in the gardening life, but spring is the primary time for restoration in the garden. Spring is also the time for restoration in the season of Lent, as we prepare our hearts for the coming of Easter. How have you found your relationship restored with God in the past? Throughout the reflections in this series?

Tuesday

Every spring when I eat the first ripe strawberry from my garden, I cry for a short time and remember my maternal grandfather. It is an annual act of remembrance that makes me feel like he is with me, even though it has been years since his death. Sometimes I wonder if the early disciples felt this way about the bread and wine after the celebration of the Last Supper, and if the ordinary means of life became bittersweet in the aftermath of the loss of their teacher and friend. Even though they knew of the resurrection, there still had to be some sense of loss, as he was no longer among them. Who have you grieved that influenced your faith? How has that sort of loss impacted you?

Wednesday

In the song "The World Was Wide Enough," the title character in the musical *Hamilton* declares, "Legacy. What is a legacy? It's planting seeds in a garden you never get to see."[13] Sometimes we plant seeds we will never see grow. How are you planting spiritual seeds for future generations beyond your own family? (Because, as Jesus points out in Matthew 5:47, even nonbelievers take care of their own.) Spend some time today contemplating your spiritual legacy in this world. Where are you planting seeds? Where might you plant seeds? What might continue to grow, even after you are gone?

Thursday

At a particularly dark time in my life, I was hiking in the mountains of Colorado. I came upon a beautiful and massive waterfall. Sitting down to rest from the hike, I noticed a tiny outcropping of rock in the middle of the waterfall. Thousands of gallons of water were rushing by this tiny outcropping every moment. And yet on this piece of rock no larger than my hand, a flower had taken root and grown. It was the answer to a prayer I had not known to pray, a promise that life can thrive even in the most drastic circumstances. How have you seen life thrive in unexpected places?

Friday

Inevitably we find "volunteers" in our garden each spring. A volunteer is a plant that we did not plant—it has grown up from seeds in our compost or from last year's produce, or on occasion, a seed will not take hold one season but will unexpectedly sprout the next. Volunteers in the garden make me think of John Wesley's concept of "prevenient grace." Prevenient grace is the grace that goes before us before we are even aware of God. How have you seen God working, in your life or someone else's, before you or that person have been aware of God's presence?

Saturday

Although I have a vague understanding of the complex biological process that turns compost into beautiful soil, I am still amazed at the beauty of God's design. What is composted has, at some point, been alive—and through composting it becomes this soil that will grow more life. Our chickens are more like pets than farm animals, and when our first chicken died, we buried her in the garden where we planned to plant tomatoes that spring. It helped me to know that she was going to be a part of the circle—not just dust to dust, but one life transforming into new life. What does the promise of new life mean for Christians? How does this promise of the life to come influence how we live this life?

Palm/Passion Sunday

TIME

Luke 19:29–40; Luke 22:66–23:56

When he had come near Bethphage and Bethany, at the place called the Mount of Olives, he sent two of the disciples, saying, "Go into the village ahead of you, and as you enter it you will find tied there a colt that has never been ridden. Untie it and bring it here. If anyone asks you, 'Why are you untying it?' just say this, 'The Lord needs it.'" So those who were sent departed and found it as he had told them. As they were untying the colt, its owners asked them, "Why are you untying the colt?" They said, "The Lord needs it." Then they brought it to Jesus; and after throwing their cloaks on the colt, they set Jesus on it. As he rode along, people kept spreading their cloaks on the road. As he was now approaching the path down from the Mount of Olives, the whole multitude of the disciples began to praise God joyfully with a loud voice for all the deeds of power that they had seen, saying,

"Blessed is the king
  who comes in the name of the Lord!
Peace in heaven,
  and glory in the highest heaven!"

Luke 19:29–38

Pilate, wanting to release Jesus, addressed them again; but they kept shouting, "Crucify, crucify him!" A third time he said to them, "Why, what evil has he done? I have found in him no ground for the sentence of death; I will therefore have him flogged and then release him." But they kept urgently demanding with loud shouts that he should be crucified; and

> their voices prevailed. So Pilate gave his verdict that their demand should be granted. He released the man they asked for, the one who had been put in prison for insurrection and murder, and he handed Jesus over as they wished.
>
> . . . When they came to the place that is called The Skull, they crucified Jesus there with the criminals, one on his right and one on his left. . . .
>
> It was now about noon, and darkness came over the whole land until three in the afternoon, while the sun's light failed; and the curtain of the temple was torn in two. Then Jesus, crying with a loud voice, said, "Father, into your hands I commend my spirit." Having said this, he breathed his last. When the centurion saw what had taken place, he praised God and said, "Certainly this man was innocent." And when all the crowds who had gathered there for this spectacle saw what had taken place, they returned home, beating their breasts. But all his acquaintances, including the women who had followed him from Galilee, stood at a distance, watching these things.
>
> Luke 23:20–25, 33, 44–49

Whiplash

The second year my husband and I were married, we got stuck at home on Christmas Day. There was a huge blizzard, and after watching several SUVs get stuck in the snow drifts on our street, we didn't even try to make it through in one of our little cars. Kansas may not be North Dakota, but we typically see a few big snowstorms each winter. The following summer, I was visiting a friend in Atlanta. The people there asked me how I was adjusting to their July heat. I smiled and politely informed them that the high at home was above 100 degrees every day that week, so the "Atlanta heat" was a lovely reprieve from the heat wave at home. Familiar with the seasonal swings in Kansas, my Atlanta friend asked me, "How on earth do you live there?"

The question, so far as it applies to weather, is a fair one. We have four distinct seasons in Kansas, but they don't change on regular calendar dates. Kansas parents must plan their children's

Halloween costumes with weather-based contingencies. One year it might snow on Halloween; another year it may be 70 degrees. It's certainly unpredictable.

While the temperature on any given date may be unpredictable, the changing of seasons is inevitable, and there is something familiar and reliable in that. But the coming and going of the seasons is how we mark the passage of time. Every year there are visible reminders of the circle of life: In the spring everything is green and lush; things continue to thrive in the summer; they begin to die in the fall; and winter is a season filled with barrenness and little life.

Because our climate is unpredictable, hard-and-fast rules cannot be followed in our region. Some years I plant my tomatoes much earlier than others. There might be an entire month's difference in when my strawberry patch gets uncovered from one year to the next. Some years we have beautiful spring mornings for Easter; other years we have snow. When we planted our first garden, my husband's grandmother became my gardening mentor. I spoke with her on a weekly basis, especially in those early years, asking over and over again, "Is it time?" In our climate, a gardener's timing is an instinct that must be cultivated over the seasons and years.

In the same way unpredictable seasons can cause climate whiplash, I also have the sense that celebrating both Palm Sunday and Passion Sunday on the same day results in liturgical whiplash. We begin the service, "Hosanna! Yay Jesus! Hosanna!" Kids come in waving palm leaves; a parade or festival atmosphere begins the service. And at some point we go from celebration mode to—bam—Jesus is dead. It's like driving 45 mph for a little while, then slamming on the brakes.

The Palm Sunday versus Passion Sunday debate puts worship leaders in a bit of a bind, torn between focusing on Jesus' triumphal entry into Jerusalem and trying to cram the whole narrative of Jesus' final week into one worship service. We know that many people will enter church on Palm/Passion Sunday and not set foot in the building again until Easter morning. Many of us feel lucky to get the attendance we do on Sunday mornings, and at times it feels like too much to encourage those attendees to come to church for two other services during Holy Week—especially when they are Maundy Thursday and Good Friday. Though vitally important, they aren't fun.

Part of me wants to just tell the story of Palm Sunday and then let the rest of the week tell the story to those there to listen. I want to have fun with kids waving palm branches, sing happy songs about Jesus marching into Jerusalem, and skip all the sad, depressing, gory parts of the story. But another part of me recognizes that the Palm Sunday festivities mean nothing without the passion that is to follow. On the one hand, how do I justify telling a story on Sunday morning that I'm just going to tell again later in the week? On the other hand, how do I justify skipping over the most important part of the story?

While struggling with this idea one Lenten season, I shared my concerns with my friend and mentor, Theresa Stewart. I asked her if it might be more emotionally responsible to let the people have their Palm Sunday without the inclusion of Passion Sunday and instead emphasize the importance of observing Maundy Thursday and Good Friday. Her response? "Plenty of pastors have been doing both on the same Sunday for centuries. I promise you, your people aren't going to be broken by a little emotional complexity." She went on to point out that the discomfort I felt was part of the point. There is, or at least ought to be, a lot of emotional discomfort through the pain of Holy Week. Why not get the ball rolling on Sunday?

The whiplash of Jesus entering triumphantly into Jerusalem, only to be immediately betrayed, arrested, and executed, makes it feel like "we're winning and losing, all in one service," as one parishioner succinctly exclaimed to me. But the paradox of both celebration and death is the heart of the Christian story. There is a concept in the field of psychology called "cognitive dissonance." It is the idea that human beings are uncomfortable with holding two disparate ideas in our minds at the same time. In other words, holding two ideas that do not merge cleanly into one another makes us squirm. But such ideas are at the foundation of Christian belief—we believe that the reign of God exists in the here and now, but we also believe it is yet to come. It is now, but it is *also* not yet. The gospel—the good news—is condensed into three succinct sentences in the Communion liturgy: "Christ has died. Christ has risen. Christ will come again." There is no celebration of Easter morning without the darkness of death that precedes it.

Jesus Enters Jerusalem

Perhaps the theme of time is perfect to encompass a day that embraces such vast dichotomies, recalling a week's worth of events in Scripture. While some may philosophize that time is "merely a human construct," no avid sports fan, music lover, or comedian can possibly buy into such nonsense—time and timing are critical in such endeavors. Simultaneously, time is fickle; a Saturday on vacation can slip by in the blink of an eye, while a Wednesday at work where nothing goes right might feel like a week. Time flies by when we are surrounded by good food and good company but slows to a crawl when we are waiting for a surgeon's report after a loved one has had surgery.

I wonder how that week felt for the crowds in Jerusalem, who within a few short days went from shouting "Hosanna!" to shouting "Crucify him!" While this sudden change in heart may seem drastic, our culture is no less fickle. Celebrities can be praised and celebrated in one news cycle, then castigated and denigrated in the next. Those on pedestals, after all, have much farther to fall.

In Jesus' time, it was common for a conquering king to ride into the conquered city on a horse—usually a fantastic warhorse. When a king entered a city outside of his own realm on a donkey, he showed that he was entering the city with peaceful intentions. Not only does Jesus enter into the city on a donkey, but he enters the city on a borrowed donkey—the "King of Kings" and "Lord of Lords" enters into Jerusalem in a humble manner.

Most pilgrims to Jerusalem would have entered on foot, so the fact that Jesus enters humbly—but in a more noteworthy fashion than the average pilgrim—is also significant. Jesus knows he is approaching the end of his ministry and the end of his life. He does get one "last hurrah" before the end in the parade-like entrance into the city. But much like in our modern era, fame is fickle. Just as we can turn from being a fan of a celebrity to greedily consuming news of that person's downfall, the cheering crowds who welcome Jesus into Jerusalem will be singing a very different tune in a few days.

In Luke 22 and 23, we see the full arc of Jesus' betrayal, arrest, and crucifixion. Jesus is betrayed by Judas, one of the disciples who has traveled with him for three years. Most people have experienced deep betrayal—perhaps not on a Judas level—but we can still understand the pain of betrayal by someone we love. The brutality of Judas greeting Jesus with a sign of friendship, a kiss, makes the betrayal sting all the more. In Judas's defense, he most likely believed he was beginning the revolution rather than ending Jesus' life. Nevertheless, the betrayal stings.

Caiaphas works behind the scenes to assure the results of Jesus' mock trial, and Pilate becomes a willing accomplice in the death of Christ. Even though, in Matthew's Gospel, he makes a show of washing his hands of the entire matter, this doesn't really cleanse him of the act of sentencing Jesus to death. How clean are we when we simply say, "I wash my hands of this," when we are exhausted from fighting for justice? What happens to the people who are oppressed when other people stand complicit with their oppressors, for the sake of "unity" or "keeping the peace"?

While some preachers, theologians, and hymn writers have spoken about Jesus being alone while he hung on the cross, all of the Gospels point to women who remained faithful and near him, or at his side. Some Gospels include his mother, Mary; others do not. But it seems appropriate to note that in a book written in a heavily patriarchal culture, when all the Gospels belabor the point that Jesus had female friends with him at the time of his death, we ought to take notice.

I have watched long, drawn-out deaths of people I love, both in my congregation and in my family. I know how slowly time can move when a loved one is suffering. The clock seems to stop, the sun seems to take years to cross the sky, the night feels as though day will never come. I imagine that those who kept vigil for the death of Jesus shared in this quirk of time perception, and that time seemed to slow to a halt. I imagine that the night felt endless as they cried themselves to sleep after his death—that there were moments they were convinced the sun would never shine again.

Anticipation

I spent a few years living in a more temperate climate during seminary. While there is not an immense difference in the latitude between

Kansas and North Carolina, the influence of the Atlantic makes a drastic difference in the climates. While part of me loved the milder weather, I also noticed that I did not appreciate or anticipate the coming of spring nearly as much. While it was wonderful to begin to see flowers bloom in the spring, the pine forests never lost their color. The world had not become the barren and brown landscape we know in Midwest winters.

Before living in North Carolina, I had dreamed of skipping winter. And now my dream had come true! While I had always thought that skipping the blistering cold months was something I wanted, spring lost some of its splendor for me in those years. For most of my life, I have lived through January and February with the anticipation that something better is on its way. There was no need for such hope-filled anticipation in a warmer climate. As the old aphorism goes, "Absence makes the heart grow fonder."

Now that I have been back in the Midwest for over ten years, there are times when I am shoveling snow or rushing through a parking lot in subzero winds when my desire to skip winter comes sneaking back. In the same way that I sometimes fantasize about skipping winter, many people want to skip Holy Week. The suffering and death of Jesus just feels like too much. I know all too well that Holy Week is not easy. Every year, the heaviness weighs me down. I begin to internalize this story I have been called to tell—because this is the darkest moment. But I encourage you to come on this journey. Without the darkness, the light of Easter morning is not nearly so bright. Without the suffering and the death, the resurrection is a shell of what it ought to be—miraculous, full of hope, and full of life.

QUESTIONS FOR REFLECTION AND DISCUSSION

1. Have you ever lived in a different climate? What was your experience of the passing of the seasons?
2. How does time pass for you? When does time go quickly? When does time move slowly? Are there moments when you lose track of time altogether? Have there been times of tragedy in your life when time has stood still?

3. What do you think about the idea of "liturgical whiplash" taking place in a worship service? What choice is made in worship at your congregation the Sunday before Easter: Palm Sunday, Passion Sunday, or both?
4. Ask your pastor why your congregation observes the Sunday before Easter the way it does. How would you choose to approach the Palm Sunday versus Passion Sunday dilemma?
5. The Scripture for this week is long, but read the full text. It gives a clear image of the crowds who shout "Hosanna!" as Jesus marches into Jerusalem and who then shout "Crucify him!" at Jesus' trial a few days later. Where do we see this fickleness of the crowds in our era? How are we a part of this? What does this tell us about fame?
6. Have Maundy Thursday and Good Friday been an important part of your spiritual journey? If so, why have they been important? If not, how do you think incorporating them into your spiritual life could change your experience of Easter?

DAILY REFLECTIONS

Monday

How do you think of time? In gardening, a few days can make all the difference; if I plant spinach and lettuce too late, they will die in the heat of summer, but if I plant my tomato plants too early, they will freeze. The gardener walks a precarious tight rope and participates in a little bit of a guessing game with the weather from year to year. How does time move in your life? How do you read time through the coming and going of the seasons? How does liturgical time impact the movement of your life?

Tuesday

Find ten minutes today for some time outdoors. If you live in a city, find some time to stroll through a park. What do you observe in nature? How do the elements of God's creation fit together? How is God speaking to you through these things?

Wednesday

I am fascinated by the feature on certain social media sites that reminds you what you posted one, two, or even ten years ago. Recently, with sleet pouring down, I was reminded that on that day a few years prior, my husband and I had been harvesting our first round of ripe strawberries. As I looked at that post, I was reminded that my strawberry plants had not even begun to flower on that same day this year. While I can offer tomato seedlings a guarantee of warmth when I start them inside under artificial light, while I can offer my parched tomato plants some water in the scorching heat of late July, I cannot control the greater shifts and whims of the weather. When you are swept up in forces beyond your control, how do you respond? Do you turn to God? Do you consider your faith?

Maundy Thursday

REMEMBER

Exodus 12:1–4, 11–14; Luke 22:14–20

The Lord said to Moses and Aaron in the land of Egypt: This month shall mark for you the beginning of months; it shall be the first month of the year for you. Tell the whole congregation of Israel that on the tenth of this month they are to take a lamb for each family, a lamb for each household. If a household is too small for a whole lamb, it shall join its closest neighbor in obtaining one; the lamb shall be divided in proportion to the number of people who eat of it. . . . This is how you shall eat it: your loins girded, your sandals on your feet, and your staff in your hand; and you shall eat it hurriedly. It is the passover of the Lord. For I will pass through the land of Egypt that night, and I will strike down every firstborn in the land of Egypt, both human beings and animals; on all the gods of Egypt I will execute judgments: I am the Lord. The blood shall be a sign for you on the houses where you live: when I see the blood, I will pass over you, and no plague shall destroy you when I strike the land of Egypt.

This day shall be a day of remembrance for you. You shall celebrate it as a festival to the Lord; throughout your generations you shall observe it as a perpetual ordinance.

Exodus 12:1–4, 11–14

When the hour came, he took his place at the table, and the apostles with him. He said to them, "I have eagerly desired to eat this Passover with you before I suffer; for I tell you, I will not eat it until it is fulfilled in the kingdom of God."

> Then he took a cup, and after giving thanks he said, "Take this and divide it among yourselves; for I tell you that from now on I will not drink of the fruit of the vine until the kingdom of God comes." Then he took a loaf of bread, and when he had given thanks, he broke it and gave it to them, saying, "This is my body, which is given for you. Do this in remembrance of me." And he did the same with the cup after supper, saying, "This cup that is poured out for you is the new covenant in my blood."
>
> Luke 22:14–20

Pecan Tree with Nine Lives

Portions of corporate memory that were taken for granted in prior centuries have been quickly lost in the span of one or two generations. My grandfather never had to call upon his own grandfather for advice in how to grow things—Grandpa spent his childhood working hard to grow food, right alongside his own parents and grandparents. I live in a very different time and place from my grandparents. My mother tells the story of how much my grandparents worried the year their potato crop died, because they weren't sure how they were going to feed their family of six through the upcoming winter. In years when my potato crop is unsuccessful, I'm frustrated and irritated, but the thought of going hungry never crosses my mind.

When my parents moved into a new house in 2002, my grandfather planted a pecan tree in their yard. That pecan tree went through the ringer: it was accidentally mowed over by a lawn-mowing service, it was eaten down to a nub by deer, it was mowed over a second time by either a neighbor or my father (depending on who is telling the story), and it has been through multiple summers of drought. The year Grandpa died, that tree had yet to produce a single pecan, even though it had been in the ground for seven years. The tree had no right to be alive, but it was death-defying in its own special way. It is a tree of restoration, a tree of resurrection. Seventeen years after my grandfather planted that tree, and ten years after his death, we harvested pecans for the first time.

As we enjoyed those pecans, we remembered my grandfather's life and the legacy he built within our family: a passionate love for

God's creation. There weren't enough pecans even for a single pie in those first few years, but the years of abundance will come. For now, we celebrate and remember.

The Jewish celebration of Passover embodies remembrance and celebration around the table. The foods our Jewish siblings share for the meal of Passover carry rich historical context and meaning; nothing on the table during the Passover feast is put there without thought, contemplation, or intention. The symbolism behind all food on the table carries the weight of the story of the exodus. And while every Jewish family will have their own recipes for the foods that fill their Passover tables, there will be many commonalities and common threads. Just as most Americans associate Thanksgiving dinner with turkey, the Passover table is filled with items that carry their own history and significance.

The passage from Exodus for Maundy Thursday carries instructions for how the Jewish people are called to remember their day of deliverance. In this passage, God prescribes the act of gathering around the table to consume lamb in the same fashion as their ancestors. It is a meal of remembrance, of acknowledging that once they were slaves in Egypt, and the power of God set them free.

The act of breaking bread together is simple and yet holy. The human tradition of gathering together at the table in celebration is not merely an act of the present; we are not just connecting to the people gathered at the table on one occasion. The traditions embodied when we gather in celebration unite those who have gone before us and those who will carry on the traditions long after we are gone.

Thanksgiving Dressing

Around the age of eight, I began making dressing (also known as stuffing—it just doesn't go inside the turkey) at my grandmother's side every Thanksgiving. She didn't have a specific recipe, just a list of ingredients: cornbread, biscuits, cream of chicken soup, eggs, onion, cooked celery, broth, salt, pepper, and sage. I still have a list of the ingredients written in her handwriting—but knowing their quantities necessitated cultivating my palate to the precise taste of what raw combination would make perfect cooked dressing. For the next twenty-five Thanksgivings, I worked at my grandma's side, learning the art of our family's dressing recipe. She told me stories from the family, keeping alive those who had taught the recipe to her. I even began growing and drying my own sage to add a special touch to the meal each year. Even in later years, when I mostly put it together by myself, she still tasted the mixture before it went into the oven and let me know what was missing.

After my grandmother passed away, I realized I was the only one who knew how to make the dressing. I began to teach the recipe to one of my cousin's children. Every Thanksgiving we work side-by-side to create this dish that is a part of our family history. I tell her stories about her great-grandmother and usually throw in a few entertaining stories about growing up with her father (my cousin) as well. Thus, the tradition is passed on from one generation to the next.

It's not really about the dressing at all. Yes, we eat it and enjoy it every year. But at this point, it's far more about the tradition, about what the meal represents. It is about the connection to the past and future of our family. It's not just cornbread dressing when we gather around the table; it takes on new meaning and becomes something more.

Here we find the heart of the Communion meal. It's not just bread and juice. That's part of what we mean by consubstantiation. Unlike my Roman Catholic siblings, my tradition does not believe that the consecrated bread and juice literally become the body and blood of Jesus Christ. However, they are more than just symbols after they are blessed; they become far more than just bread and juice. The Communion table connects us to all the saints who have gone before us, all Christians around the world at present, and all those who will bear the faith and carry the cross of Christ in the future. We are connected to these persons through the Table. We are connected to the Divine through the physical act of sharing the bread and the cup; the curtain between the holy and the ordinary is torn in two, and we feast upon the grace we have been offered.

In Luke 22, Jesus sets the precedent for what will become the Christian Communion service, also sometimes referred to as the Great Thanksgiving. The act of Jesus giving thanks is central to this passage of Scripture, so much so that it is specifically mentioned two separate times, both when Jesus takes the cup and when he takes the loaf of bread. Acts of thanksgiving are, in and of themselves, acts of remembrance as we remember to give thanks and glory to God.

Oatmeal-Coconut Cookies

Across cultures, most people have a food that specifically reminds them of childhood, or a food that they identify with the word "home." I once knew, deep in my soul, that a romantic relationship wasn't going to work out because the boy I was dating couldn't stand the taste of my grandmother's oatmeal-coconut cookies; you must like these cookies to truly be a part of my family.

When my grandmother died, in addition to being the pastor at her funeral, I also had another special task for the day of the ceremony: It was my job to bake several batches of Grandma's oatmeal-coconut cookies. After the funeral and the graveside service, we returned to the church my grandparents had helped build. Before lunch began, I gathered with my cousins to partake in Grandma's cookies. When I serve Communion to small children, I make sure I am at eye level with them, and I tell them, "Jesus loves you very much!" When I passed out cookies to my cousins' children, I held out the cookies and told them each, "Grandma Owsley loves you very much." I have thought about the parallels of these acts on countless occasions since that day. Yes, it was food, not actual love. But the love that those cookies symbolized was powerful, tangible, and delicious. The cookies symbolized a rich history—the years we spent with our grandmother, who was stern and solemn yet whose love we never questioned.

The love we find at the Communion Table through partaking of the bread and cup is more than an act of remembrance. Through the sacrament, we acknowledge and renew the covenant made through baptism, we acknowledge and renew the grace of Jesus Christ at work within us. Even though Jesus knew that Judas would betray him within hours, he still broke bread with him; Jesus still offered Judas grace. Much like Judas, we never come to the table with our hands clean; rather, we find ourselves in need of constant renewal and forgiveness.

Just as the flavor of my grandmother's cookies evokes remembrance of her love, I cannot help but feel God's love through the smell and taste of Communion. As a child, I loved the flavor of Communion so much that one day I decided to pour myself a glass of grape juice and dip a piece of bread into the juice. Although I knew the bread and juice were the same brands we used at church, I was surprised when they didn't seem to taste the same. I couldn't name what wasn't right, but dipping the bread in juice by myself at the kitchen table simply didn't offer the same satisfaction as when I did the same thing at church.

At that age I did not have words for complicated theological concepts around Communion, words such as "consubstantiation" or "sanctification." However, it seemed as though even my taste buds recognized this wasn't the real thing; rather than delightful deliciousness, all I tasted was very soggy bread. As a child I didn't have a formal understanding that Communion is meant to be an act in community. After all, both words share the common Latin root *communis*, meaning "common, or shared by many." But perhaps something deeper within me understood that something important was missing when I tried to replicate the sensations of Communion by myself. Communion is an act of remembrance of Jesus' love for us, but also of the love shared in community. If I could go back and explain it to my childhood self, the simplest explanation might be this: "Bread is best when it's shared."

QUESTIONS FOR REFLECTION AND DISCUSSION

1. What are the foods that unite your family, community, or church? What are the tastes and flavors that take you back to a childhood place or memory?
2. Why do we continue to prepare the same dishes and delights year after year? What role do food memories have in our collective psyche?
3. Do some research into a traditional Passover service. What are the uniting dishes that every Passover celebration will have? How are these presented?
4. In many Protestant denominations, Communion is considered one of only two sacraments (the other being baptism). Why is Communion held in such high regard?

5. Do you remember the first time you received Communion? If so, what was the experience like? If not, what is your first memory of receiving Communion?
6. What are you called to remember this year during Holy Week? What acts of remembrance might inspire you as we approach Good Friday and Easter?

Good Friday

FAST

John 18:1–19:42

Meanwhile, standing near the cross of Jesus were his mother, and his mother's sister, Mary the wife of Clopas, and Mary Magdalene. When Jesus saw his mother and the disciple whom he loved standing beside her, he said to his mother, "Woman, here is your son." Then he said to the disciple, "Here is your mother." And from that hour the disciple took her into his own home.

After this, when Jesus knew that all was now finished, he said (in order to fulfil the scripture), "I am thirsty." A jar full of sour wine was standing there. So they put a sponge full of the wine on a branch of hyssop and held it to his mouth. When Jesus had received the wine, he said, "It is finished." Then he bowed his head and gave up his spirit.

Since it was the day of Preparation, the Jews did not want the bodies left on the cross during the sabbath, especially because that sabbath was a day of great solemnity. So they asked Pilate to have the legs of the crucified men broken and the bodies removed. Then the soldiers came and broke the legs of the first and of the other who had been crucified with him. But when they came to Jesus and saw that he was already dead, they did not break his legs. Instead, one of the soldiers pierced his side with a spear, and at once blood and water came out.

John 19:25b–34

Feast or Famine

My husband and I occasionally joke that the trouble with growing a lot of our own food, and trying to eat food in season, is that we often find ourselves in "feast or famine" mode. When those first tomatoes get ripe in the summer, we can't get enough fresh tomatoes. But by the time I start canning them and turning them into sauce to freeze, we are very tired of eating fresh tomatoes at all our meals. When the first strawberries ripen each spring, we are careful to dole them out evenly and make sure we each have the same number of berries. By the time strawberry harvest is over, my husband is starting to get tired of strawberries. (I think I could eat strawberries fresh from the garden every day for the rest of my life and never grow tired of them.) But this is what we mean by feast or famine. Trying to eat what is in season in our part of the world means that we are constantly in a space of scarcity or abundance.

A quick trip to a large grocery store will reveal that America has food in abundance, if a person can afford it. We have the option of buying strawberries or blueberries in February regardless of the fact that there is snow on the ground. But let me tell you a secret you probably already know: not everything that looks like a strawberry tastes like a strawberry. Despite Driscoll's best attempts, nothing from the supermarket can come close to the taste of a strawberry straight from the garden in May—nothing.

After several years of establishing our strawberry plants, we began to have plenty to share, so I took a huge container of freshly picked strawberries when I went to visit my cousin and his family. When my cousin tasted them, a look of sheer delight came over his face. "This is it! This is it!" he announced joyfully to his wife. He explained to me (and his wife confirmed) that for his entire adult life, he had been searching for the strawberries he remembered from childhood. He longed for the strawberries we had picked and eaten straight from our grandfather's garden.

After years of searching, he had begun to believe that he simply remembered these strawberries with "rose-colored" glasses. He had become convinced that the berries we enjoyed in childhood were just ordinary strawberries, misremembered as spectacular through his adult perspective.

What was the secret to growing strawberries like my grandfather? The only real secret is in the variety of strawberries. The breed of strawberries my grandfather grew, and the strawberries I therefore grow, have been bred for taste. The strawberries in the grocery store have been bred for size, ship-ability, and shelf life. They are a product that can be shipped from as far away as South America. You will only find the variety of strawberries I love in local gardens and farmers markets. They are small and are best eaten or preserved within a day or two of picking. Have I purchased strawberries out of season? Of course I have. But the flavor of those February strawberries is more like the vague memory of strawberries rather than the real deal.

So why spend so much time on Good Friday talking about strawberries? Because our culture does with life what agriculture has done with strawberries. Our culture tries to make all things available all the time. I am an Amazon Prime member and frequent shopper, and I love that I can buy anything I want and have it shipped directly to me within two days. But one result of living in a culture that tells us we can have whatever we want whenever we want it is that we have little patience for ideas like fasting or contemplation. We learn to believe that the vague memory of strawberry flavor is "good enough," when it will never replace the real thing. We begin to believe that getting something right when we want it is always a good thing.

Practicing Patience

I recently had lunch scheduled with a friend. I arrived a few minutes early, so after being seated, I reached in my purse to pull out my cell phone; it just made sense to use the time wisely and reply to a few work emails while I waited. I immediately realized I had left my cell phone at home. I sat for a few moments, looking around the restaurant and feeling a little lost. How on earth was I going to pass the time? Our scheduled meeting time wasn't for another ten minutes! What if my friend was running late, and I had to sit idly for fifteen or even twenty minutes?

I am an "old" millennial. This means I am in the generation raised with access to modern technology, but technology also grew rapidly while I was growing up. I was in my early twenties by the time I got my first smartphone. I have an abundance of life experience in waiting patiently for another person without having access to Wi-Fi. But patience and waiting are learned behaviors, and like all learned behaviors, they must be practiced or they can be easily forgotten.

Cultivating a space for people to practice patience and waiting is a critical part of Holy Week (and Advent, but that's another study). Good Friday reminds us to slow down, make space and time for waiting, and to cultivate the practice of patience.

A few days before my nineteenth birthday, I ate the best piece of apple pie I have ever had. I had been in the hospital for several days after my shoulder surgery that had not gone as planned, and all I had eaten for three days had been crackers, ice chips, and off-brand Sprite. On day three of my stay, the nurse brought me a slice of apple pie and a cup of ice cream. As I ate it, I kept telling my mom it was the best apple pie I had ever eaten. I even had her try a bite. In the midst of her caring for her very sick daughter, she said, "That's pretty good." But a few weeks later, when I brought up how great the pie at the hospital had been, she said, "Kara, I think it's because you hadn't eaten in three days. In all honesty, it was just crappy hospital food." I was shocked! How could she not agree that that was the best apple pie in the world?

When we went back to the hospital for a follow-up visit, I insisted on stopping in the cafeteria and getting some pie and ice cream. I'm sure you can guess what comes next. Mom was right. It was crappy hospital food. The crust was soggy, there wasn't nearly enough spice, and the pie filling was more like goo than apples. But the waiting, the anticipation of food, the complete lack of food for three days all made it taste like one of the best things I had ever eaten. While I logically know that slice of pie probably wasn't that good, one of my baking goals is to achieve an apple pie so delicious that it can live up to that memory.

My point is this: Sometimes waiting can be a wonderful thing. Sometimes waiting makes something even better when we finally have it. In the case of Good Friday, living in the space of despair and darkness will make the light shine that much more powerfully on Easter morning. The light isn't nearly as beautiful if it is not preceded by the darkest of nights.

Embracing Discomfort

Like most pastors I know, I like to leave people feeling warm and fuzzy at the end of my sermons. I like the sermons I preach and the dinner parties I host to end in the same way: people leave feeling happy and full. But this is not the only call of a pastor—and certainly not the call of a prophet. Sometimes, like it or not, it is my job to let people leave worship in discomfort. Sometimes I can't (and shouldn't) neatly tie the bow on the sermon. Good Friday might be the occasion on which this is the most appropriate.

We are called to discomfort as we hear the story of Christ's death on the cross once again. On Good Friday I fight my normal urge to throw in some hope or promise into even the most prophetic of sermon topics. Good Friday is about despair—and that's okay. Anyone who has lived for a little while has experienced despair, and it is not something we talk about in the church very often. Here is a day set aside to acknowledge the deepest and darkest places of the human soul.

As someone who has struggled with eating disorders and ministered to those also struggling with eating disorders, I do not emphasize fasting from food. Inviting (or especially commanding) a food fast for a person in recovery from an eating disorder is akin to inviting a recovering alcoholic to drink a few shots of tequila as a spiritual practice; it is a recipe for disaster. I have also seen too many people treat Lent as a personal diet plan in the hopes of losing weight, rather than treating it as a spiritual practice: "I'm giving up chocolate" or "I'm giving up sweets." I do talk about fasting, but I emphasize all the ways in our lives we can choose to fast that have nothing to do with food: a day to fast from social media, a day to fast from television, a day to fast from caffeine, and so forth.

I often encourage church members to give up something for Lent—an expensive daily cup of coffee, eating out, trips to the movies, a daily soda—and then donate whatever money they would have spent on those things to the church's chosen mission project for Lent. In this way, it's not just about giving something up; it's also about giving to the mission of the church. I have also known people who offer up a fast of their time during Lent by adding something to their schedule each day. When I encounter individuals interested in this approach, I usually suggest adding a devotional, prayer, or other spiritual practice during the season. Either way, the change in habit is meant to cause a bit of discomfort.

Sometimes my husband or I will find random packets of seeds in the garage or basement left over from previous years. We often don't remember precisely how old those packets are, but usually, once planted, those seeds will grow. As long as they are kept comfortable in a dry and dark place, the seeds will remain in seed form. The seeds don't grow until I remove them from that dry and dark comfort, place them in wet earth, and coax them forth with light. In my culture, there is a lot of value placed on productivity. There is a prevailing cultural myth that the busier a person is, the more inherent value that person must possess. Therefore, there is often a lot of discomfort in offering up additional time during the day. Much like the seeds removed from their comfortable dormancy, removing ourselves from the comforts of ordinary routine can inspire growth.

Growth and discomfort often go hand in hand. Whether it is a child experiencing pain during a growth spurt, or the spiritual revelations that take place when we are suffering, we rarely grow out of comfortable places. When we are well-fed, all our needs are met, and we are satisfied, our souls tend to stay dormant, like the seeds inside the packet. Humans rarely find spiritual growth while residing in such places of contentment. However, spiritual growth often grows out of the fertile soil of human discomfort. Do we intentionally seek pain and suffering? Of course not. For most people, just living life will bring plenty of opportunities for growth.

It Ends in the Garden

The Gospel of John outlines Jesus' crucifixion in excruciating detail. When I have used today's suggested reading in worship, my parishioners have been surprised that I use such a long text in the Good Friday service. I do break the text up between multiple readers and in multiple sections throughout the service. But sometimes it's best to go back to the original story—Good Friday is a moment when the best sermon might be letting the Scripture speak for itself.

The lengthy text takes us through Judas' betrayal, Peter's betrayal, and the betrayal of the same crowds who had shouted "Hosanna!" when Jesus entered the city now shouting "Crucify him!" The text walks through Mary's pain at watching her son crucified, and Jesus' command to the "disciple whom he loved" to care for his mother. We watch as Pilate struggles with handing down a death sentence, and our hearts ache as Jesus breathes his last breath. We even see Jesus' body taken down from the cross, and witness the body being laid in a tomb.

The stories I tell throughout this book contain lessons from gardening that illustrate the spiritual aspects of journeying through Lent. When I began writing, it did not immediately occur to me that the entirety of the Good Friday lectionary text began and ended in a garden, but it is a happy coincidence. Jesus is arrested in a garden while praying, the beginning of the Scripture for Good Friday. Toward the end of the reading, Jesus' body is laid to rest in another garden where there is a tomb. Historians have written that the "garden" referenced in this text bears little resemblance to the plot of land where I grow my tomatoes and strawberries. While agriculture was obviously a major industry for many people in the ancient world, and many people likely had gardens not that dissimilar from my own, "garden" in this usage is more similar to what we would call a park. A green space, perhaps with a pool (or fountain, in our time) with intentionally planted trees. These parks were places of peace, set apart from the sounds and smells of city life—the same purpose that parks serve in our large metropolises today.

It makes sense that there would be a tomb in such a place, when taking into consideration the places our culture buries our dead. Often cemeteries have a park-like presence, including benches and places to sit, manicured green spaces, sometimes with paths to walk on, and beautiful trees. Several cemeteries I have been to even have lovely large ponds on the premises. But the tranquility of the place where Jesus' body is laid, much like the tranquil graveyards where our own loved ones are buried, does not soften the pain of his death.

On Good Friday, worship usually ends with Jesus' death, and those who participate leave worship with the last words spoken being the heartbreaking news that Jesus is dead and growing cold in the tomb. The fasting and waiting called for in this time is uncomfortable and unnerving, much as the grief must have been for Jesus' friends and followers on that first Good Friday. But like seeds that have been removed from the safety of their package and buried in the earth, we bury Jesus each Good Friday with the knowledge that on the other side of this discomfort and waiting, something beautiful will grow.

QUESTIONS FOR REFLECTION AND DISCUSSION

1. Have you ever eaten produce the same day it was picked? What has that experience been like? What differences were there in flavor, appearance, and texture? If you have not eaten fresh local produce, research ways you might be able to acquire some during the spring and summer months.
2. What is the difference between surface faith and deep faith? Why is it important to struggle with deep questions and difficult passages of Scripture? What does it mean that Good Friday forces us to wait for the happy ending?
3. How might having a day of grief and mourning in the church be a good thing? What does it mean that we acknowledge that we all have moments of utter despair and darkness? What benefit can Christians find in confronting this truth of the human experience in a spiritual manner?
4. What do you think about the options for fasting presented in this chapter? Have you ever participated in a form of fasting? What was that experience like?
5. What is it like to walk out of church on Good Friday, leaving Jesus dead in a cold tomb? How can this change the experience of Easter morning?

DAILY REFLECTIONS

Day 40 (Holy Saturday)

Rise
We scatter seeds with hope,
digging deep in dark earth,
soaking soil with sweat,
believing that—eventually—the days of harvest will arrive.

Will the sun shine? Will the rains come?
Will storms destroy? Will hail fall?
All of these are forces beyond our control.
So, we say a prayer of blessings
sprinkling soil over seeds,
and place our faith in the promise:

what is buried will rise.

Easter Sunday

FEAST

John 20:1–18

> But Mary stood weeping outside the tomb. As she wept, she bent over to look into the tomb; and she saw two angels in white, sitting where the body of Jesus had been lying, one at the head and the other at the feet. They said to her, "Woman, why are you weeping?" She said to them, "They have taken away my Lord, and I do not know where they have laid him." When she had said this, she turned around and saw Jesus standing there, but she did not know that it was Jesus. Jesus said to her, "Woman, why are you weeping? Whom are you looking for?" Supposing him to be the gardener, she said to him, "Sir, if you have carried him away, tell me where you have laid him, and I will take him away." Jesus said to her, "Mary!" She turned and said to him in Hebrew, "Rabbouni!" (which means Teacher). Jesus said to her, "Do not hold on to me, because I have not yet ascended to the Father. But go to my brothers and say to them, 'I am ascending to my Father and your Father, to my God and your God.'" Mary Magdalene went and announced to the disciples, "I have seen the Lord"; and she told them that he had said these things to her.
>
> John 20:11–18

Garden Feast

During my childhood, my family often traveled to my maternal grandparents' house when it was time to help with harvesting the bounty of Grandpa's garden. After carefully instructing us in our task, Grandpa handed us buckets for the harvest, reminded us what to look for in ripe fruit, and showed us where we should begin picking strawberries, blackberries, or whatever was being harvested that day. Surrounded by family, we moved up and down the rows, the soft thump of fruit landing in the buckets as they were gathered. (I confess that when I was harvesting blackberries or strawberries, far more fruit wound up in my mouth than in the bucket.) Most family members helped in the garden, but a few stayed inside the house and helped my grandmother can or freeze whatever was being harvested that day. As my grandparents did not have air-conditioning, most people preferred to be outside and under the hot Missouri sun in August rather than in the kitchen with canning pots filled with boiling water.

When the day's hard work was finished, we gathered for the evening meal, or what is called "supper" in that region. The table was laden with food to reward us for a hard day of work, and it always contained fresh versions of whatever delicious delights were in season. Whether it was corn on the cob that had been picked and shucked an hour before dinner, sliced tomatoes that had only been off the vine for a few hours, or fried zucchini that had been collected earlier in the day, we shared in the feast of the garden's bounty.

Across cultures and around the world, feasting is frequently associated with celebrations. The Christian tradition is no exception. While many of our churches are known for potluck dinners (usually with four different types of Jell-O salad here in the Midwest), pancake breakfasts, or spaghetti suppers, the feast tradition at the center of our faith takes place in Communion. While the complex theology around Communion is often one of the things that divides denominations, the importance of gathering around the bread and cup at the table remains fundamental within Christian traditions.

Inclusion in the Feast

When I was in seminary, I memorized the intellectual reasons my tradition serves Communion to people of all ages. I went to one of my mentors and shared with him that while I could explain the theology behind serving children Communion, it still made me uncomfortable.

I struggled to fully wrap my mind around the meaning of Communion, How could a child possibly understand the importance and weight of participating at the Communion table? He then said something that became fundamental to my theology: "There is no way a three-year-old can grasp what Communion means. She can't comprehend the powerful significance we give to the bread and the cup. She knows nothing of theories of consubstantiation or redemption or grace. But you know what every child will understand? She will understand if she has been left out."

A person might not understand the feast, but all human beings can tell if they are being left out of a celebration. No one should ever walk away from Jesus' table hungry—ever. On Easter morning we break the spiritual fast of Lent. We celebrate the miraculous.

This understanding has led me to believe that incorporating children into the service of Communion is life-giving for a congregation. In one church I served, I began a tradition of having the children serve Communion. The first time I asked two of our girls, ages eight and nine, to help serve, they were excited and nervous. Just before worship began, I had them repeat the words they were supposed to say: "The body of Christ, broken for you," as the bread was distributed, and "The blood of Christ, shed for you," as the cup was offered. One girl was so nervous that she was mumbling the words nearly inaudibly as she passed out the bread. I put a hand on her shoulder and said softly, "I've heard you be a lot louder than that! Speak up!" They both did a spectacular job for the rest of the people coming through the line. As soon as the service was over, I turned around to see them flying down the aisle to beat the crowd that greets me as the congregation leaves the sanctuary. They both stopped when they got to me and asked, almost in unison, if they could help serve Communion again at the next service. I haven't heard too many children beg their parents to stay for a second round of church, but these girls had caught a glimpse of the glory of Jesus' feast. They wanted to experience it again.

One Sunday as I was serving Communion, I noticed a child in the congregation receive the elements and then run around the perimeter of the sanctuary to come back up the aisle to receive Communion from the other station. After church, he guiltily confessed to me that he had taken Communion twice. He was shocked by my answer:

"That is *awesome*!" He looked at me a little confused. "You can have as much Communion as you want! More Communion! More grace! I wish everyone in our church was that excited about the sacraments!" The next Communion Sunday, he led two younger boys in the same path; the little trio received Communion at one station and circled back to the other line and received Communion again. After the service, a concerned adult approached me. "I don't think you saw, since you were serving Communion, but that group of boys took Communion twice," he said. "I know!" I replied. "Isn't it awesome that they are that excited about Communion?" He muttered, "Hmpf" and walked away. I didn't intend my response to his concerns to be sassy or sarcastic; I really was excited that they were that eager about receiving the sacrament.

Am I so naive that I didn't know that those boys mostly just loved the bread we use in Communion? Of course not. I recognized that it was a game, or that they wanted another bite of the delicious bread we serve. But perhaps they may have caught a glimpse of the gospel of abundance in the feast of the Communion Table.

No One Leaves Hungry

Whenever I prepare food for others, I am always concerned that everyone has enough. During the years I worked in campus ministry, the ministry didn't own its own property. We worshiped in the student union on campus, but for other events and activities we usually met at my house. Over the years my students learned through experience a truth that became spoken among them: "No one leaves Pastor Kara's house hungry." Whether they hadn't had a chance to eat between class and work that day, had their wallet stolen and couldn't buy their lunch, or didn't have any food in the house they were going home to, no one left my house hungry. I always had a snack when we gathered, but if students showed up and informed me they hadn't eaten all day, I would either find some leftovers, heat up a meal I had frozen, or whip something up using whatever was in the pantry and fridge. Sometimes I cleaned out the pantry, fridge, and freezer to send food home with a student that I knew had no food at home.

Other times I took the student grocery shopping on the campus ministry's account. I have no idea how much food I fed these students over the years. But I did my best to make sure no one ever left my home hungry.

While this applies to feasting in the literal sense, I also think it applies spiritually as well. A motto for our churches ought to be "No one leaves Jesus' house hungry." In a spiritual sense I think we are always going to be hungry for more. But it still applies, especially when we gather around the table.

The tradition of the potluck in many churches is strong in this sense. I served one church that had a potluck after worship one Sunday a month. We had a new family come to visit on a potluck Sunday, and I invited them to come downstairs and join us for lunch after worship. The adults quickly said they couldn't possibly join us because they hadn't brought a dish to contribute. I assured them there would be more than enough. When we finally made it downstairs and they saw the buffet line spread out across several tables, one of the kids turned to me and said, "More than enough—you weren't kidding!" While many churches can be overly miserly concerning budgetary matters, I have seen the gospel of abundance play out at church potlucks time and time again. There is plenty for everyone.

Jesus lived out this reality through more than one story in Scripture. Whether it was multiplying the loaves and fishes to feed a huge crowd, or turning water into wine at a wedding celebration, Jesus understood the value of an excellent feast. In both stories there was more than enough for everyone, with some left over.

What Mary Saw

The resurrection passage from John is my favorite from the Gospels. I know I'm not really supposed to have a favorite version, but I love the way John tells this story. Perhaps, as a woman in ministry, I am drawn to the fact that Mary is the first person to spread the gospel—literally "good news"—that Jesus has risen from the dead. Mary is the first person to preach the gospel of Jesus Christ. How could a female pastor not be drawn to this empowering story?

But I also love the way the story is told. John is a master storyteller. I can feel the weight in Mary's chest as she makes her way to the tomb, only to find it empty. I can feel the breathlessness of the disciples as they race to confirm what they have been told: Jesus' body is missing. I can feel Mary's despair as she sits outside the tomb, believing everything she loved and lived for is lost.

Countless gallons of ink have been used by theologians arguing why Mary does not recognize Jesus when he approaches her in the garden, with theories ranging from the angle of the sun in Mary's eyes to the assertion that Jesus' appearance changed after the resurrection. I confess that I find these lines of argument to be a waste of time. I firmly believe that Mary would have recognized the risen Christ if she had been looking for him.

The Gospels do not contain the story of celebration that follows the resurrection of Jesus. We do not know what sort of party Mary or the disciples threw after seeing Jesus risen from the dead. But based on what I know of humankind, I suspect some feasting was involved as they rejoiced in the hope of resurrection, as they rejoiced in the promise that death does not have the final word. I believe there were a number of celebrations when those who followed Jesus realized that love won, after all.

In the Eastern Orthodox Church there is a tradition on Easter morning. The priest stands before the people and says, "Christ is risen," and the people respond, "Christ has risen indeed." They repeat this three times. I have adapted this tradition on Easter mornings in the churches I serve. I like to remind people every year, toward the end of Easter worship, that their job is not to hoard the good news of Jesus Christ. Every baptized Christian has committed to sharing this good news with the world. When I close with the repeated call and response, the first response of "Christ is risen indeed" is inevitably very Midwestern polite. I remind people that this is the good news, that this deserves cheers like those we use at sporting events and great concerts. As Christian people, the good news comprises all that we are! And so, as their voices get louder with each consecutive "Christ has risen indeed," I look forward to their final chorus as they loudly proclaim Jesus' victory over the grave, and our own as well. It's a feast for my ears.

QUESTIONS FOR REFLECTION AND DISCUSSION

1. Describe a memorable feast from your past. What made the occasion memorable? What food was served? Why were people gathered together? Why does it stand out in your memory?
2. How might we see Communion through the amazed and excited eyes of the children in the stories mentioned? How can we become that excited about coming to the table?
3. What is meant by "gospel of abundance"? How might approaching life with the good news of abundance, rather than the fear of scarcity, bring good news to our churches? Communities? Homes?
4. How can we ensure that no one leaves Jesus' house hungry? What can feasting look like in your life and in your community?
5. How will you respond to the gospel, the good news of Jesus Christ, with a resounding "Christ has risen indeed"?
6. How have you grown through this Lenten season? What have you learned? Have you felt called to make any changes in your life? If so, what are they?

Resources for Worship Leaders

*T*his book can be used in a churchwide worship series during the season of Lent. Below are ideas for two community spiritual practices the entire church can participate in, as well as suggestions for each holy day, including sermon starters, liturgy for worship, prompts for children's time during worship, and ideas for altar arts. Some sections also have an additional suggestion for worship that fits the theme for the day. These resources can be adapted to fit the needs of a specific congregation, and I encourage you to do so. Let your creativity take flight (or assign this task to someone else) to make these suggestions a unique experience tailored to the needs of your community.

Community Spiritual Practices

- Choose a cause or nonprofit that is important to your community, or an organization that partners with your church. For the season of Lent, encourage church members to give up one place where they spend money. This can be purchasing coffee on the way to work, a weekly trip to the movies, or eating out a few times a week. Ask people to donate the money they would have spent in other places to the church's chosen cause or organization. Remind people to pray as they make this sacrifice.
- On Ash Wednesday or the First Sunday in Lent, add an additional element to the worship service. Purchase enough small terra-cotta planters for everyone in worship to receive one. Fill them with potting soil in advance. Invite people to come forward as a part

of this service, and offer each person a seed and a planter, saying, "God makes beautiful things out of dust." Invite them to plant their seeds and then watch them grow. Remind people of their seedling throughout the season. Gungor's "You Make Beautiful Things" in the background is an excellent musical accompaniment during this part of the service. Empty any leftover planters of potting soil, and pass them out to children to decorate with permanent markers. These extra planters can be used for decoration or for visitor and homebound gifts on Easter Sunday.

Ash Wednesday

Scripture: Joel 2:1–2, 12–17; Matthew 6:1–6, 16–21

Theme: Soil

Sermon Starter: "From dust you have come and to dust you shall return." Another word for "dust" is "soil." Just as proper soil cultivation is the foundation of a successful garden, God is concerned with how we cultivate our souls. Joel calls for communal repentance after the exile. Jesus reminds us that our motivations in repentance matter as much as the acts of repentance themselves. What communal repentance needs to take place in your community or church? Are some of those things you can name? How can people repent or "turn around" to realign themselves with God? Resist the urge to leave your congregation feeling too cozy after the sermon, but also consider how you will offer up the hope of God's grace amid the need for repentance.

Altar Arts: Begin with burlap over the altar. Add a large, empty terra-cotta planter, positioned on its side. Since the planter will most likely be round, prevent rolling by putting some hymnals or extra books strategically around the planter, underneath the burlap. Make sure your planter is secure. Add a single piece of brown shimmery tulle coming out of the planter. Flow the tulle all the way onto the chancel area if there is space.

Children's Time: This is one of the rare occasions I choose not to do a children's time. However, if there are children present, I try to make them a part of the service by helping serve Communion or distributing ashes.

Liturgy

Invitation to the Observance of Lent

Today is a call to fast, to recognize the patterns of God's creation,
to recognize the order of the Christian year.
The time of feasting will come.
But now we empty our hearts,
we spring-clean our souls,
we prepare for the journey to come.
In a world that seeks to fill our lives
with instant gratification of every desire,
we recognize God's call to set ourselves apart,
to enter into a spiritual season of famine.
We empty ourselves in this season,
preparing for the great feast to come
in the brilliance of Easter morning.

Call to Worship

Merciful God, we are but dust.
But as the abundance of the earth displays,
You can do phenomenal things with dust.

From the daisy to the redwood,
from the strawberry to the apple tree,
from the tamarind to the tomatillo,
You fill this world with beauty and splendor,
with life beyond our wildest imaginations.

We know that if we open our hearts and minds,
You, Creator God, will do phenomenal things through us.

Prayer of Confession

We have heard the trumpets of Zion,
and know that the day of the Lord is drawing near.
But even now, O God, you have called us to return to you,
for you are slow to anger, and abounding in steadfast love.
Help us choose the path that leads to repentance.

God, all too often we have practiced our piety in public,
basking in the glory of our fellow human beings.

Remind us to turn our faces toward you,
knowing that our reward for faithfulness is in heaven.
Help us choose the path that leads to repentance.

We have stored up treasures on earth;
trinkets that mean nothing when judgment comes.
Tonight we pause, acknowledging that we are but dust,
and one day to dust we will return.
Help us choose the path that leads to repentance.

We confess we have often run from our own mortality,
regardless of the cost. Help us to run toward you.
Give us courage to remember how fleeting this life is,
and that we must therefore devote our all to you.
Help us choose the path that leads to repentance.

Litany of Penitence

With confidence in God's mercy,
let us pray for the world and for ourselves, saying,
God, in your mercy,
hear our prayer.

For the church, that in this season of fasting and repentance
the people of God may recognize their detachment
from God's creation and seek to restore the Creator's justice.
God, in your mercy,
hear our prayer.

For a world in which peace seems unreachable,
that the nations might seek peace with one another.
God, in your mercy,
hear our prayer.

For the leaders and powerful persons of the world,
that they might lead with integrity,
and be imbued with respect for all of creation.
God, in your mercy,
hear our prayer.

For the city/town of ____________ and all who live here,
that neighborhoods might be places
where all good things are free to grow.

God, in your mercy,
hear our prayer.

For the least, last, and lost,
that they may be delivered from their distress.
For God's people, that we might hear their cries.
God, in your mercy,
hear our prayer.

For all these things, and those known only to you,
we pray in the name of Jesus Christ our Lord.
Amen.

Blessing of the Ashes

Bless, O God, these ashes and those who receive them.
From dust we were created, and to dust we shall return.
Let these ashes remind us of our sin and our mortality,
of our desperate need for your love and your grace.
May they serve as a reminder that in your generous spirit,
you make beautiful things out of dust,
and grow beautiful things in us.
Amen.

Benediction

From dust you have come, and to dust you shall return.
But God can make beautiful things out of dust.
Amen.

First Sunday of Lent

Scripture: Genesis 2:15–17; 3:1–17; Luke 4:1–13

Theme: Order

Sermon Starter: The order and organization of a garden matters. God has ordered humanity: to live fully is to live in God, to turn from God's created order is to live in sin. The order is disrupted by Adam and Eve in the garden of Eden; Jesus restores God's order by resisting temptation in the desert. How does your tradition define sin, and how might you offer that explanation in a discussion of Adam and Eve's fall from grace? How does Jesus, as the new Adam and new Eve, provide an example of what humanity might have been and might become?

Altar Arts: Leave the planter and brown tulle as they were on Ash Wednesday.

Children's Time: Before the service, dig up some worms from your garden or yard. (If this is not an option in your climate during this time of year, go to a local bait shop and purchase live worms.) Encouraging each child to be gentle, give them all an opportunity to hold a worm if they desire. Discuss what it means when worms live in the garden. How are they good for the soil? What do they do in the garden? What is their purpose in a healthy garden? Discuss how God has ordered the world—so that even things that are a little slimy and gross like worms have an important place in the order of life.

Liturgy

Opening Prayer

We gather in this Lenten season knowing we are broken.
Come and be seen.

We gather in this Lenten season knowing we need forgiveness.
Come and be heard.

We gather in this Lenten season knowing our hearts long for God.
Come and be loved.

We gather in this Lenten season knowing God calls us all.
Come as you are.

Prayer of Confession

God, all too often we have turned from you,
and our love has failed.
Our longing for glory
has blinded us to the joy of your ways.
Help us choose the path that leads to life.

We have turned aside and put our faith in things,
in people, in institutions.
We have placed our hope in the mortal, the tangible, the finite
rather than placing our hope in you.
Help us choose the path that leads to life.

We have embraced hatred, sorrow, and anger
instead of your life-giving love.
We have sown seeds of discord
rather than creating communities where love abounds.
Help us choose the path that leads to life.

We long to turn our faces toward you,
away from death and destruction.
We long to be people of love, light, and grace,
that we might be your beacons in a desperate world.
Help us choose the path that leads to life.

Give us strength to glory in your creation,
to celebrate the beauty and wonder you have made.
Give us strength to reclaim the promise of Christ's life,
to claim the promise of Christ's love.
Help us choose the path that leads to life.
Amen.

Second Sunday of Lent

Scripture: Genesis 15:1–12, 17–18; Mark 8:31–38

Theme: Life

Sermon Starter: Life in general is messy and complicated, and both the gardening life and the spiritual life are no exceptions. Abram and Sarai must enter into the messiness of beginning life anew, and Jesus speaks in paradox, saying, "For those who want to save their life will lose it, and those who lose their life for my sake . . . will save it." How do those who start life anew adapt to the challenges of the mess, and how can the church help them through this process?

Altar Arts: Add a small piece of shimmery green tulle to the planter display. You can roll up and fold over a piece of tulle, securing it with a rubber band, to make it look like a plant shooting out of the earth.

Children's Time: Ask the children what it takes for them to stay alive and grow. What are the things that they need to live? Look for the basics: water, food, shelter, clothes. Next, ask if they know what the word "thrive" means. Explain that "thrive" means to live life to its fullest. What does it take for them to thrive? If they have trouble coming up with ideas, offer a few: love, hugs, education. Discuss what it takes for people to thrive in their relationship with God.

Liturgy

Opening Prayer

We gather in this Lenten season knowing we are broken.
Come and be seen.

We gather in this Lenten season knowing we need forgiveness.
Come and be heard.

We gather in this Lenten season knowing our hearts long for God.
Come and be loved.

We gather in this Lenten season knowing God calls us all.
Come as you are.

Prayer of Confession

Our Heavenly Creator,
you have called us to heavenly things.
You have called us to be born of the spirit,
to live into the birth of our baptism.
Help us choose the path that leads to new life.

As you called Abram and Sarai out of their homeland,
so, too, you call us to new and unexpected places.
The mysteries of the Holy Spirit
call us to new and unexpected journeys.
Help us choose the path that leads to new life.

Jesus spoke in paradox,
proclaiming that those who wished to save their lives
must give up their lives and follow him.
Grant us strength to take up our crosses and follow.
Help us choose the path that leads to new life.

Give us power to bathe once more
in the waters of your baptismal font;
give us strength to remember we are
blessed so that we might bless others.
Help us choose the path that leads to new life.
Amen.

Third Sunday of Lent

Scripture: Psalm 63:1–8; John 4:5–42

Theme: Water

Sermon Starter: All life on this planet requires water to survive. Water is life. Water is an integral part of both gardening and sacrament. The psalmist cries out to God, desiring to seek God as the thirsty long for a drink of water. Jesus speaks to the Samaritan woman about "living water" she can drink so as to never be thirsty again. How is water a justice issue in your community? In the nation? Around the world? What are the significance of and the theology of baptism in your tradition?

Altar Arts: Add a pitcher or bowl to the altar and arrange two different colors of blue shimmery tulle flowing out of the pitcher or bowl. Flow them out into the chancel area or onto the ground if there is space.

Children's Time: Bring a large bowl filled with water to the front of the church. Ask the children what could be done with the water. When they have given all the answers they can think of, ask, "Can we *play* in the water?" and make the biggest splash you can with your hands. Encourage them to also play in the water. Talk about how important water is for life. Why does water matter? How can we conserve water? How can we take good care of God's creation?

Special Addition to This Service: The benediction for this service is simply speaking the lyrics of the first verse of "Come, Thou Fount of Every Blessing." Take the bowl of water from the children's time and walk down the aisle, throwing handfuls of water onto the congregation as you deliver the benediction.

Liturgy

Opening Prayer

We gather in this Lenten season knowing we are broken.
Come and be seen.

We gather in this Lenten season knowing we need forgiveness.
Come and be heard.

We gather in this Lenten season knowing our hearts long for God.
Come and be loved.

We gather in this Lenten season knowing God calls us all.
Come as you are.

Prayer of Confession

God, we confess that we have often
rejected the call of our baptisms.
Too often we have accepted the forces of wickedness
and embraced the evil powers of this world.
Help us choose the path that leads to love.

We have forgotten the covenant we made
to resist evil, injustice, and oppression
in whatever forms they present themselves.
We have forgotten the promises of baptism.
Help us choose the path that leads to love.

We long for you as the thirsty long for water.
We recognize our souls need you for survival,
just as our bodies need water for survival.
Give us strength to name our weakness.
Help us choose the path that leads to love.

May we be forgiven, may we turn toward you.
May we remember and reclaim

the promise made through the Holy Spirit
in the blessing of baptismal waters.
Help us choose the path that leads to love.
Amen.

Fourth Sunday of Lent

Scripture: 1 Samuel 16:1–13 and John 3:14–21

Theme: Light

Sermon Starter: Light is essential to our existence. As the garden depends on sunlight to thrive, we depend on light to illuminate the world around us. God turns on a light so Samuel can see and anoint King David, and Jesus proclaims that those who do good will be drawn toward the light. What keeps drawing human beings back into the darkness of night? How might people be encouraged toward the light of Christ?

Altar Arts: Leave the terra-cotta pot with the tulle from the previous weeks. Wind a yellow piece of tulle around the other pieces on the altar to represent light. If you have enough space, add a glass lantern and have the yellow tulle emerging from the lantern.

Children's Time: Ask the children about a time when they experienced darkness. What was it like? Were they afraid? How did they respond? Where were they? Now ask why the sun is important to life. Could anything grow without sunlight? Why is it important to have light? Discuss how light is important in seeing and how God can help us see things more clearly—what it means when grown-ups talk about "shedding light on a situation."

Liturgy

Opening Prayer

We gather in this Lenten season knowing we are broken.
Come and be seen.

We gather in this Lenten season knowing we need forgiveness.
Come and be heard.

We gather in this Lenten season knowing our hearts long for God.
Come and be loved.

We gather in this Lenten season knowing God calls us all.
Come as you are.

Prayer of Confession

Our Heavenly Creator, all too often we see as the world sees
rather than looking at life through heaven's eyes.
Help us to see with your vision,
help us to see with your wisdom.
Help us choose the path that leads to light.

Like Samuel, we fail to see value in others.
As Jesus' miracle granted sight to the blind man,
restore our vision to see your creation, our fellow creatures,
and our fellow human beings as you see them.
Help us choose the path that leads to light.

When we feel overcome by darkness,
help us to look to the light of the world.
May we choose to turn our faces toward the light,
time and time and time again.
Help us choose the path that leads to light.

Give us wisdom, God of creation,
to see potential where others see despair,
to seek grace where others seek revenge,
and to see love where others see only hate.
Help us choose the path that leads to light.
Amen.

Fifth Sunday of Lent

Scripture: Ezekiel 37:1–14; John 11:1–45

Theme: Restoration

Sermon Starter: Sometimes, despite all the odds in the garden, life finds a way. Ezekiel experiences a vision in which he witnesses the rebirth and growth of his nation, and Lazarus is resurrected from the dead. The restoration of life is possible through the goodness of God. How can restoration create ripple effects? What is broken in your community that needs to be restored? How can your church help?

Altar Arts: Add a long, flowing piece of green tulle to the terra-cotta planter with the other tulle, replacing the sprout piece of green tulle.

Children's Time: Ask the children how big babies are. How much have they themselves grown since they were little babies? Have them show you how much they have grown. How do they know they have grown? Do their clothes and shoes fit differently? Can they reach things they couldn't reach before? Let them know that as their bodies continue to grow, so will their faith, and that even after our bodies stop growing our spiritual lives never should.

Liturgy

Opening Prayer

We gather in this Lenten season knowing we are broken.
Come and be seen.

We gather in this Lenten season knowing we need forgiveness.
Come and be heard.

We gather in this Lenten season knowing our hearts long for God.
Come and be loved.

We gather in this Lenten season knowing God calls us all.
Come as you are.

Prayer of Confession

God Almighty, all too often we choose the way of despair.
All too often we choose to live in darkness and death
rather than seeking your light, love, and grace.
Help us to see possibility in the life you offer us.
Help us choose the path that leads to restoration.

We are but empty bodies until you breathe into us the breath of life.
Like the army of Ezekiel's vision,
breathe into each of us the breath of life.
Fill this place with the power of your Holy Spirit.
Help us choose the path that leads to restoration.

Like Mary and Martha,
we are often filled with doubt and sorrow.
Open our eyes to the miracle of your creation.
Open our eyes to the miracle of your re-creation.
Help us choose the path that leads to restoration.

As Jesus resurrected Lazarus from the dead,
so you can resurrect what needs to live within us.
We pray for the way of life, for the way of love.
Guide us in all things, O Giver of Life.
Help us choose the path that leads to restoration.
Amen.

Palm/Passion Sunday

Scripture: Luke 19:29–40; Luke 22:66–23:56

Theme: Time

Sermon Starter: Time and timing matter. As the gardener follows the arc of the seasons, Palm/Passion Sunday invites us into the full arc of Holy Week emotions, rejoicing in Palm Sunday and mourning the death of Jesus all at one time. Jesus enters Jerusalem triumphant, but a short time later he is arrested and then crucified on the cross. How might the highs and lows of this Sunday be incorporated in such a short time?

Altar Arts: A few weeks in advance, put out a call to the congregation to see if someone would be willing to lend the church a mantle clock. Make sure the chimes are all turned off. Arrange the mantle clock on the altar around the terra-cotta planter. Flow a piece of orange tulle around the clock. Place the Christ candle on the altar.

Children's Time: Greet the children, then after they have sat down and settled down, begin staring straight ahead silently. When they finally ask what you're doing, shake your head like you're waking yourself up and say, "Sorry! I lost track of time. Have you ever lost track of time?" Ask them if they have had experiences where time goes by really fast, and others when it seems to creep by at a snail's pace. Ask if the time is really going faster or slower, or if that's just how they perceive it. Talk about how it is important that we give ourselves time to think about Holy Week as we journey toward Easter Sunday.

Liturgy

Opening Prayer

We gather in this Lenten season knowing we are broken.
Come and be seen.

We gather in this Lenten season knowing we need forgiveness.
Come and be heard.

We gather in this Lenten season knowing our hearts long for God.
Come and be loved.

We gather in this Lenten season knowing God calls us all.
Come as you are.

Prayer of Confession

God Almighty, creator of all things,
You are the source of our life, the source of our light.
And yet all too often we fail to stop and pause,
we fail to acknowledge our need for you.
Help us choose the path that leads to the cross.

The world spins so fast, and we find ourselves
easily caught in the whirlwind of chaos.
Help us, on this Sunday of Palms,
to take time to look to you.
Help us choose the path that leads to the cross.

We long for quick fixes, for cheap miracles,
rather than taking the time to seek your face.

We chase after what is easy and what is fast
rather than seeking what is difficult and what is everlasting.
Help us choose the path that leads to the cross.

Give us wisdom to seek the slower way this week,
that we may take our time on the journey to the cross.
Grant that we may journey through this Holy Week,
with all our hearts, all our souls, and all our minds.
Help us choose the path that leads to the cross.
Amen.

Maundy Thursday

Scripture: Exodus 12:1–4, 11–14; Luke 22:14–20

Theme: Remember

Sermon Starter: We have foods that are precious in our memories with family, friends, and even across entire cultures. What are those foods for you? For your congregation? The Passover feast is a remembrance of God's deliverance of the Hebrew people from slavery in Egypt. Jesus gathers around the table with the disciples to celebrate Passover and initiates the practice that will become our Communion liturgy. How is Communion a uniting act of past, present, and future? How do we remember through ritual, liturgy, and tradition?

Altar Arts: Remove everything from the altar except the cross, candles, and Communion elements. Weave a piece of dark red tulle around the elements on the table. While this is a starkly bare altar arrangement, it is fitting for the middle of Holy Week. Furthermore, Communion ought to be the center of worship on Maundy Thursday; if that's all that is on the altar, it cannot help but be the focal point.

Children's Time: Ask the children if there are certain foods that make them think of certain occasions or memories. Ask them to list the foods they associate with specific holidays. If they are having trouble dreaming up answers, offer a few prompts: turkey on Thanksgiving, birthday cake on birthdays. Ask why we eat the same things at special occasions. What makes an occasion special? Why do we do the same things year after year to mark a certain event? Encourage them to think about Communion as a meal that is worth remembering.

Liturgy

Opening Prayer

We gather on this Maundy Thursday knowing we are broken.
Come and be seen.

We gather on this Maundy Thursday knowing we need forgiveness.
Come and be heard.

We gather on this Maundy Thursday knowing our hearts long for God.
Come and be loved.

We gather on this Maundy Thursday knowing God calls us all.
Come as you are.

Prayer of Confession

God Almighty, creator of all things,
You have gathered us here and called us to remember.
Give us the patience to stop and pause,
to recall how you have been at work in the history of our people.
Help us choose the path that leads to remembrance.

As the angel of death passed over the lamb's blood
marking the doorposts of faithful Hebrew people,
assure us that through the sacrifice of Christ,
death will pass us by as well.
Help us choose the path that leads to remembrance.

As Jesus gathered with his disciples, his friends,
they remembered the occasion of that first Passover.
As we break bread and drink of the cup,
may we remember the occasion of that Last Supper.
Help us choose the path that leads to remembrance.

As we journey toward the difficulty and pain of the cross,
may we embrace the path laid out for Jesus, our Savior.

May we enter the darkness with confidence
that you walk with us, even in the hour of death.
Help us choose the path that leads to remembrance.
Amen.

Good Friday

Scripture: John 18:1–19:42

Theme: Fast

Sermon Starter: Good Friday is a time to fast and to embrace the discomfort of the story of the crucifixion. Times of fasting increase our appreciation of the feast. Much like the theme for this series, this passage from John begins and ends in a garden. How can discomfort help us grow? What is the importance of fasting and waiting, especially with the speed of modern culture?

Altar Arts: Take everything off the altar except for the candles, the cross, and the terra-cotta planter. Leave the planter empty. Place the Christ candle on the altar.

Children's Time: I usually forgo the children's sermon on Good Friday. Very few parents tend to bring their children to this service anyway.

Liturgy

Opening Prayer

We gather on this Good Friday knowing we are broken.
We know we are broken.

We gather in this Lenten season knowing we need forgiveness.
We know we need forgiveness.

We gather in this Lenten season knowing our hearts long for God.
We long for God.

We gather in this Lenten season knowing God calls us all.
We wait for God.

Pastoral Prayer

God, we confess we do not like to contemplate suffering and loneliness.
But when Jesus was suffering the most, he was also the most alone.
As Peter denied Jesus three times on the night of the crucifixion,
let us acknowledge and name the ways we have also abandoned Jesus.
Help us choose the path that leads to Christ.

In an era of constant amusement, we do not want to be bored.
In an era of substances that will keep us from pain, we do not want to suffer.
Allow us to enter this time of reflection, this time of fasting,
to comprehend Jesus' sacrifice and death for us all.
Help us choose the path that leads to Christ.

When we are thirsty, we have water regularly available.
When we are hungry, we are quickly sated.
Give us strength to find redemption in the wanting,
and help us to find you in the midst of suffering.
Help us choose the path that leads to Christ.

When we hear the story told one more time
of Jesus' last words—"It is finished"—
may we feel Jesus' hopelessness and sorrow.
May we dwell in that space of sorrow this day.
Help us choose the path that leads to Christ.
Amen.

Prayer of Confession

God our Creator, the Master Gardener,
we cry out to you this night and beg that you,
in your infinite mercy, would hear our prayer.
Tonight is the winter solstice of the Christian year,
the longest and darkest night of the soul.

The joy of Jesus' command to "love one another"
is still fresh on our lips from Maundy Thursday.
But the taste of the bread and the juice has grown sour on our tongues, in bitter mockery of yesterday's feast.

We are culpable in the tragedies of Good Friday,
our hands are also stained with Christ's blood.
How many times have we stood in Judas's stead,
betraying Jesus (and our fellow human beings)
with symbols of friendship and love?
All too often we have walked Judas's path.

How often have we stood in Simon Peter's place,
denying Jesus (and our fellow human beings)
with our words and our actions?
Far too many times we have followed Simon Peter's example.

All too frequently have we argued over rags,
while Jesus (and our fellow human beings)
have been stripped, beaten, and abused.
Over and over we have been the soldiers at the foot of the cross.

From dust we have come and to dust we shall return.
But in this moment in between, we cry out.
Open our eyes to your glory, O God,
show us where we have turned aside from your tears,
open our ears that we may hear the cries of your creation.
Amen.

Easter Sunday

Scripture: John 20:1–18

Theme: Feast

Sermon Starter: When it is time to harvest what has grown, we feast. Today we reap the harvest of the journey of Lent. On Easter we celebrate the resurrection of Christ and join in the celebration feast of Communion. How might embracing the gospel of abundance change our lives? Our churches? Our communities? Our world? How might we offer more feasts out in the world?

Altar Arts: Leave the Christ candle. Leave the burlap; you do not want gorgeous white altar cloths on the altar with all the dirt that is going to be up there. Have a second terra-cotta planter that is identical to the one on the altar on standby. Fill this planter with potting soil and then flowering plants and greenery. Before worship on Easter, swap out the empty planter with the full one. (Having a second planter for this step is not essential, but it may help alleviate some stress in Holy Week.) Take all of the smaller terra-cotta planters left over from the first Sunday and plant flowers in them (for our climate and this time of year, pansies tend to be a good choice.) Add all of these smaller planters to the altar at different heights and levels. Wind all the colors of tulle from throughout the series around the planters and the Christ candle. Invite guests to Easter services to take one of the smaller planters home with them. If there are any left over, deliver them to church members who are homebound or in nursing homes.

Children's Time: Bring a special food treat for the kids at children's time. This can be cookies from a special recipe, and the person who baked them can explain why the recipe is special. It can also be ordinary Easter candy. (Be sensitive to allergies, whatever you choose.) Discuss what food traditions and "feasts" surround our special days. Ask the children what foods they associate with special occasions. They might mention Thanksgiving turkey, birthday cake and ice cream, and barbecue on the Fourth of July. Talk about why we gather to celebrate Easter, and why this is a day of "feasting" in our spiritual lives.

Special Addition to This Service: If your tradition allows visitors to receive Communion, make sure to emphasize that everyone who wants to follow Jesus is welcome to receive, regardless of their membership in your church or any church. (This is especially important on Easter with so many visitors.) Serving Communion at Easter is not traditional in my denomination, but the theme for the day is "feast"!

Liturgy

Opening Prayer

We gather this Easter morning knowing we are broken.
We know we are seen.

We gather this Easter morning knowing we need forgiveness.
We know we are heard.

We gather this Easter morning knowing our hearts long for God.
We know we are loved.

We gather this Easter morning knowing God calls us all.
We come as we are.

Prayer of Confession

We journeyed through the season of Lent,
we feasted together at the Passover table,
and we grieved together at the foot of the cross.
We thank you, God, as we gather in joy this Easter morning!
Help us choose the path that leads to resurrection.

We, like Mary Magdalene, often fail to see
when the Risen Christ stands before us.
We ask, God, that you open our eyes
to your presence in our midst.
Help us choose the path that leads to resurrection.

Like the disciples running to the tomb,
we often fail to believe what you have revealed to us.
Give us wisdom to understand the gospel,
the good news of Jesus Christ.
Help us choose the path that leads to resurrection.

We rejoice on this Easter morning,
celebrating Jesus' triumph over the grave.
We rejoice in the stone that has been rolled away,
granting us everlasting life in Christ.
Help us choose the path that leads to resurrection.
Amen.

A Time to Grow Communion Liturgy

The Lord be with you.
And also with you.

Lift up your hearts.
We lift them up to the Lord.

Let us give our thanks and praise.
It is right to give our thanks and praise.

It is a beautiful thing to give thanks and praise to you, Almighty God.
In the beginning, you formed the cosmos, and gave birth
to the brilliant sun that warms our earth.
You formed the clouds that bring rain,
the oceans that crash,
the snow that falls.
Out of the dust of the earth you created
the trees that tower, grass that grows,
and every type of plant that sustains the animals of this planet.
You are the true master gardener,
providing for all forms of life on our earth.
Creator of all things, you shaped humankind
from the dust and formed us in your image,
breathing into us the *ruach*, the breath of life.
You formed us to be in union with you,
as our Creator, and in balance with the entirety of your creation.
But we turned from the path that leads to you, and our love failed.
But you, in your everlasting mercy, remained steadfast.
You continued to provide, continued to love,
and continued to make covenant with us, your broken creation.
And so we join with all of creation (for even the rocks must cry out)
in singing your unending praise.

Holy, holy, holy Lord,
God of power and might.

Heaven and earth are full of your glory.

Hosanna in the highest.

Blessed is the one who comes in the name of the Lord.

Hosanna in the highest!

In the fullness of time, you sent your son Jesus to dwell among us.
Your spirit anointed him to preach good news to the poor,
to proclaim the release of the captives,
and to set at liberty those who are oppressed.
Jesus announced the time had come
when you would save your people.
He healed the sick, fed the hungry,
and joined in suppers with sinners just like us.
He turned water into wine at the wedding in Cana,
cursed the fig tree in a fit of hunger,
and multiplied the loaves and fishes to feed the hungry masses.
By the baptism of his suffering, death and resurrection,
you delivered us from the slavery that is sin and death
and made a new covenant with us to be our God.
When Jesus ascended, he promised to remain with us always
in the power of your Word and Holy Spirit.
On the night in which he gathered with his disciples,
he took the bread
and gave thanks to you for your sustaining work in the world.
He broke the bread, offered it to his disciples,
and said, "Take, eat. This is my body, given for you.
Do this in remembrance of me."
After the meal had ended, he took the cup,
once more gave thanks to you, and offered it to his disciples,
saying, "Drink from this, all of you;
this is my blood of the new covenant,
poured out for you and for many for the forgiveness of sins.
As often as you drink of it, remember me."
And so, in remembrance of these your mighty acts in Jesus Christ,
we offer ourselves as a holy and living sacrifice,
in union with Christ's offering, as we proclaim the mystery of faith:

Christ has died. Christ has risen. Christ will come again.

Pour out your Holy Spirit on us gathered here
and on these gifts of bread and wine.
Make them be for us the body and blood of Jesus Christ,
that we might be for the world the body of Christ, redeemed by his blood.
By the sweat on the brows of our human siblings
has the grain been harvested to prepare this bread.
By the work of laborers in the fields have the grapes
been harvested to prepare this cup.
Even in this, Almighty God, we are complicit in the injustices of this world.
We confess to you and pray that you would open our eyes and our hearts.
May we serve as vessels of your justice,
may we speak on behalf of those who are not heard,
may we use our places of privilege
to stand against oppression in whatever forms it presents itself.
By your spirit, work within us,
that we might be examples of hope and grace
in a world so desperately in need of you.
While we work toward making your reign a reality here on earth,
we look toward the day when we will gather together
and feast at your heavenly banquet.
All honor and glory are yours, Creator God, now and forever.
Amen.*

* Adapted from "A Service of Word and Table I," in *The United Methodist Hymnal* (Nashville: United Methodist Publishing House, 1989), 9–11.

Acknowledgments

*I*f everything in my life had gone according to my plans, this book would never have been written. Thanks be to God who can turn both literal and metaphorical manure into beautiful things.

Thanks to my parents, Ken and Wanda Eidson, who have always believed in me and encouraged me. Thanks to my sister, Kelli Cooper. When I tell Kelli "I don't know how to do that," her favorite response is, "Then learn." Thanks to my family members for reading, editing, and reviewing my early drafts.

I am grateful to my childhood pastor, Rev. Adam Hamilton, and youth director, Dan Entwistle, who shaped my faith from an early age. Thanks to Adam for your support through the years and your encouragement to publish this book.

Thanks to my campus minister, Rev. Paul Smith, who helped guide me toward healing and a deepened faith in God and who encouraged me to accept my call. Thanks to Kelly Utley, who encouraged me to write.

I am forever grateful for my professors at Duke Divinity, especially Dr. Amy Laura Hall and Dr. Esther Acolatse, who influenced and shaped my identity as a Christian and as a pastor. My friends from seminary still keep me on track from across the miles; thanks to Blair, Jenn, and Sarah.

This book would not have been possible without the support, guidance, and mentoring of Teresa Stewart. I was a pain in the behind when I sat through my first seminar with her, but she loved me anyway. Her love is a lot like God's love in that way.

Thanks to Edie Snethen, my spiritual mentor, who keeps me on track with my relationship with the Divine.

Amy Saunders, my friend and farmer, has taught me so much and allowed me to spend precious sabbath time on her farm. Thanks to the entire Saunders family for letting me reconnect to God through time on their land.

Thank you to the congregations of Spring Hill United Methodist Church and Crestview United Methodist Church. Pastoring both congregations helped me develop the themes and ideas in this book. Thank you to the Institute community for reminding me of God's call on my life and giving me the opportunity to share God's love.

Thank you to the team at Westminster John Knox Press, especially Jessica Miller Kelley, Julie Tonini, and the whole marketing team. I am grateful for your guidance, patience, and wisdom.

Last, but most important, thank you to my husband, Michael Lee. I love the ongoing adventure of our mini-farm, garden, and our beautiful life together. He encourages me to keep writing, keep writing, keep writing. When life gives us manure, he is always able to see the beautiful things that can grow from it.

Notes

1. Two excellent albeit very different resources on soil depletion are Diana Butler Bass, *Grounded: Finding God in the World: A Spiritual Revolution* (New York: HarperOne, 2015), and Gene Logsdon, *Holy Shit: Managing Manure to Save Mankind* (White River Junction, VT: Chelsea Green Publishing, 2010).

2. United States Environmental Protection Agency, "Composting at Home," accessed March 22, 2021, https://www.epa.gov/recycle/composting-home.

3. Lisa and Michael Gungor, "Beautiful Things," *Beautiful Things*, Brash Music, 2010.

4. Diana Butler Bass, *Grounded: Finding God in the World: A Spiritual Revolution* (New York: HarperOne, 2015), 42.

5. *The Lion King*, directed by Roger Allers and Rob Minkoff, Walt Disney Pictures, 1994.

6. Tovia Smith, "As Milk Prices Decline, Worries about Farmer Suicides Rise," National Public Radio, February 27, 2018, https://www.npr.org/2018/02/27/586586267/as-milk-prices-decline-worries-about-dairy-farmer-suicides-rise.

7. USDA, "Food Waste FAQs," accessed March 22, 2021, https://www.usda.gov/foodwaste/faqs.

8. Barbara J. McClure, *Moving beyond Individualism in Pastoral Care and Counseling* (Eugene, OR: Cascade Books, 2010), chap. 7, Kindle.

9. Mike Crawford and His Secret Siblings, "Words to Build a Life On," *Songs from Jacob's Well, Volumes 1 and 2: Even the Darkness Will Not Be Dark to You*, Jacob's Well Records, 2008.

10. Kathleen Norris, *The Quotidian Mysteries: Laundry, Liturgy, and "Women's Work"* (New York: Paulist Press, 1998).

11. "The Baptismal Covenant I," in *The United Methodist Hymnal* (Nashville: United Methodist Publishing House, 1989), 33.

12. "A Christmas Carol," *Dr. Who*, BBC Cymru Wales, December 25, 2010.

13. Lin-Manuel Miranda, "The World Was Wide Enough," *Hamilton* (original Broadway cast recording), Atlantic Records, 2007.

Made in United States
North Haven, CT
15 February 2022

16131194R00076